CULTURAL RESOURCE MANAGEMENT PROGRAM
Division of Continuing Studies
University of Victoria
PO Box 3030 STN CSC
Victoria, BC V8W 3N6 Canada

DA660.P47

UNDERSTANDING OUR SURROUNDINGS

5·5·5
·6
17
18

Founded in 1957, the Civic Trust is a recognised charity supported by voluntary contributions. It encourages the protection and improvement of the environment. By means of conferences, practical projects, films and reports it focuses attention on major issues in planning and architecture. It publishes a bi-monthly journal and maintains a library and photographic collection. It makes Awards for good development of all kinds. Among some particular concerns have been the initiation of co-operative street improvement schemes; the promotion of new techniques for transplanting semi-mature trees; industrial dereliction and urban wasteland; the problems of damage and disruption caused by heavy lorries. The Trust encourages the formation of local amenity societies and gives advice and support to over 1,250 such societies now on its register. Its proposals led to the creation of the Lee Valley Regional Park Authority. It was closely associated with the drafting of the Civic Amenities Act 1967, which created the concept of the Conservation Area, and of the Town and Country Amenities Act 1974. At the request of the Government, it provided the United Kingdom Secretariat for European Architectural Heritage Year 1975. It administers the Architectural Heritage Fund, which provides loan capital to local buildings preservation trusts; on behalf of the Historic Buildings Council, government grant aid to non-outstanding conservation areas; and also on behalf of the Department of the Environment, the work of the Heritage Education Group. Associate Trusts are linked with it in the North West, the North East, Scotland and Wales.

CIVIC TRUST
17 CARLTON HOUSE TERRACE LONDON SW1Y 5AW (01-930 0914)

Civic Trust for the North West
56 Oxford Street, Manchester M1 6EU (061-236 7464)

Civic Trust for the North East
34/35 Saddler Street, Durham DH1 3NU (0385 61182)

Scottish Civic Trust
24 George Square, Glasgow G2 1EF (041-221 1466)

Civic Trust, Wales/Treftadaeth Cymru
46 Cardiff Road, Llandaff, Cardiff CF5 2DT (0222 552388)

UNDERSTANDING OUR SURROUNDINGS

a manual of urban interpretation
by Arthur Percival

CIVIC TRUST

ISBN 0 900849 95 9 APRIL 1979

Published by the Civic Trust ©
17 Carlton House Terrace London SW1Y 5AW (01-930 0914)

Typeset and Printed by Tonbridge Printers Ltd, Tonbridge, Kent

Contents

Acknowledgements

Michael Middleton and Victor Rose were
responsible for design and made many helpful
suggestions. Others who gave generously of
their time and expertise in offering assistance
were:

  Professor T C Barker (*London School of Economics*)

  Gillian Brown (*Civic Trust for the North West*)

  Michael Glen (*formerly of British Tourist Authority*)

  Peter Landon

  Geoffrey Lord (*Carnegie United Kingdom Trust*)

  C A Parrack (*Leek & District Civic Society*)

  Keith Pennyfather (*Countryside Commission*)

  Andrew Pierssené (*Norfolk Heritage*)

  Peter Rogers (*Civic Trust for the North East*)

  Valerie Thom (*Countryside Commission for Scotland*)

*Publication of this book has been made
possible by a generous loan from the
Carnegie United Kingdom Trust, to which
the Civic Trust takes this opportunity of
expressing its appreciation.*

Introduction

Many of us, in these days of foreign travel, have very little notion of the treasures of art and history which still live in the towns and villages of our own country. And many of us have not fully grasped the truth how largely in every land national history is made up of local history.

Edward Freeman, *English Towns and Districts, 1883*

In recent years the term 'interpretation' has been adopted, first in National Parks and nature reserves and then in museums, to describe systematic efforts to ensure that people learn as much as possible from their visits and are encouraged to find out more for themselves.

The expert's immediate aim is to share his knowledge and insight so that others can share his enjoyment; his underlying objective, to win support for the measures needed to protect and conserve for the benefit of posterity the resources in his custody. 'Through interpretation, understanding; through understanding, appreciation; through appreciation, protection', as an American pioneer of interpretation has succinctly put it.*

This kind of interpretation, in itself, is nothing new. For centuries it has been the stock-in-trade of guidebook-writers, poets, painters, vergers, custodians and even gardeners—like the Earl of Shaftesbury's who in 1661 showed Pepys round Hatfield House, 'the chappel with brave pictures, and . . . the gardens, such as I never saw in all my life; nor so good flowers, nor so great gooseburys, as big as nutmegs.'**

What is new about interpretation is that over the last few decades it has been applied increasingly to develop appreciation of features, particularly in the countryside, the significance of which might otherwise go unnoticed by the public at large. The object—already being achieved—is to stimulate a more acute public concern that habitats should not be destroyed and the balance of nature upset.

Unfortunately the same attention has been given only fitfully to the *human* habitat—the settlements where we live, work, shop and relax. Whether in consequence or not, very many have

been wantonly ruined over the last thirty years and their social and economic equilibrium upset. Communities have been broken up; whole areas reduced from modest prosperity to bleak deprivation; whole neighbourhoods razed to the ground regardless of any environmental qualities they possessed. The nation is slow to learn; while it wrestles with the aftermath of such changes, new damage is still being done elsewhere. If further blunders of this kind are to be averted, we need to ensure—through interpretation—that human habitats are better and more widely understood.

The scope is vast. In many cities, towns, villages and hamlets the fabric still faithfully mirrors the community's development from the remote past to the present day; and wherever change has been organic people in the know can have a lot of fun simply piecing the clues together, often using their experience to make new discoveries.

But for many people detective work of this kind is impossible because they have never been shown how to tackle it. Those of us who have gained an idiomatic command of the language of towns have a responsibility to pass it on to others so that they may share our enjoyment. Indeed we *need* to pass it on if there is to be widespread support for the conservation of what is worthwhile in our surroundings and the improvement of what is not.

Let it be clear at the outset that these considerations apply everywhere—in the suburb no less than the village, the industrial town as well as the picture-book conservation area. The heritage of an area is everything in it left to us by the past, including the recent past. Even in the bleakest modern suburb there are usually features of interest, sometimes also of charm. Tenuously linking it with the rural society, from which most of us are only a few generations removed, may be a farm cottage or two, a barn, perhaps even a common or village green. The street pattern will probably reflect the phases in

*Freeman Tilden, Interpreting our Heritage, University of North Carolina Press, 1967.
**Samuel Pepys, Diary, 22 July 1661.

which it was built up, and possibly the constraint of a stream or beck now culverted. Street and pub names may be revealing, and so too may the contrast in design and layout between public and private housing. There may be a disused cinema converted into a supermarket (two minor social revolutions epitomised in one building), a motor showroom on the site of a smithy, or an old beerhouse doing game duty as the 'Tudor Bar' of the chic pub which has superseded it.

But there is more to urban interpretation than tracing change and adaptation. Any balanced human habitat depends for its social and economic equilibrium on a framework of components, complex, interdependent and unique to itself. There are the employment base, the service industries, the residential provision, and the welfare, social and cultural facilities. Subtract one of the bigger components, or too many of the smaller ones too quickly, and the framework loses its strength and stability. It has happened too often when big factories close, for example; when a glossy new shopping centre leaves an old High Street derelict; when 'housing renewal' is synonymous only with the planned destruction of neighbourhoods which need rehabilitation rather than rebuilding. Ignorance is often to blame. We were not taught in school about the way communities evolve, we have failed to learn since how their vitality can be sapped by maltreatment and amputation. In consequence we have often set about a watchmaking job with all the refinement of a pile-driver.

Urban interpretation must therefore try to explain how towns *work.* At one level this means simply saying what is made in a particular factory, which hinterland a school serves, from what area a shopping centre draws its clientele. At another it means explaining what particular contribution a factory makes to the local economy, how a particular hospital meets an essential local need, why a particular rail service receives a subsidy. Considerations such as these are too often taken for granted.

Thus in an urban setting interpretation seeks to give people an insight into the way a community has evolved, and continues to evolve, to meet changing social and economic needs. It enables them to see for themselves how this evolution can be 'read' in the existing land-use pattern, street plan and fabric. Where a locality or community is specially attractive to resident, worker and shopper, interpretation can identify the qualities which make it so. With the new insight it gives them, people are better equipped to play a constructive part in maintaining a healthy human habitat, with decent environmental standards, wherever they live or work—in the area concerned, or 200 miles away.

The purpose of this manual, therefore, is to suggest some techniques for the interpretation of the urban settlements which, in Britain, form the greater part of the human habitat. None of the techniques is new, though of some there is not yet much experience in an urban setting. What are common to all are certain principles, and these are discussed next.

BOOKS TO READ

Most available books discuss interpretation in a rural setting. However many of the techniques they describe are also valid for cities, town and villages.

Elizabeth Beazley, **The Countryside on View,** Constable, 1971, (paperback Triskel/Christopher Davies Publishers Ltd, 1975)

Countryside Commission, **Interpretive Planning** (Advisory Series No 2), 1977, *free*

Countryside Commission/Countryside Commission for Scotland, **Guide to Countryside Interpretation:**

Part I: **Principles of Countryside Interpretation and Interpretive Planning,** by Don Aldridge, HMSO, 1975
Part II: **Interpretive Media and Facilities,** by Keith Pennyfather, HMSO, 1975

Society for the Interpretation of Britain's Heritage Newsletter (published three times a year and available to members only; contains much useful information about current projects—details from the Society's Secretary, Martin Orrom, 9 Greenhill Gardens, Edinburgh EH10 4BN)

Grant W Sharpe, editor, **Interpreting the Environment,** John Wiley & Sons, 1976

Freeman Tilden, **Interpreting Our Heritage,** University of North Carolina Press, 1967

Highlighting aspects of the town's heritage is this display (mounted by Wakefield City Council) in a 'shop window' under the Town Hall at Pontefract (above left). Good starting point for visitors to the site of the Battle of Bosworth Field (1485) is this information centre created in a disused station by Leicestershire County Council (above right). Strategically sited in the town's market place, this bookshop gives visitors to Ironbridge the opportunity of enriching their enjoyment of the town's history (below left). A temporary display, as here in a shop window at Leek (below right), helps to engender civic identity and may pave the way for a permanent heritage centre.

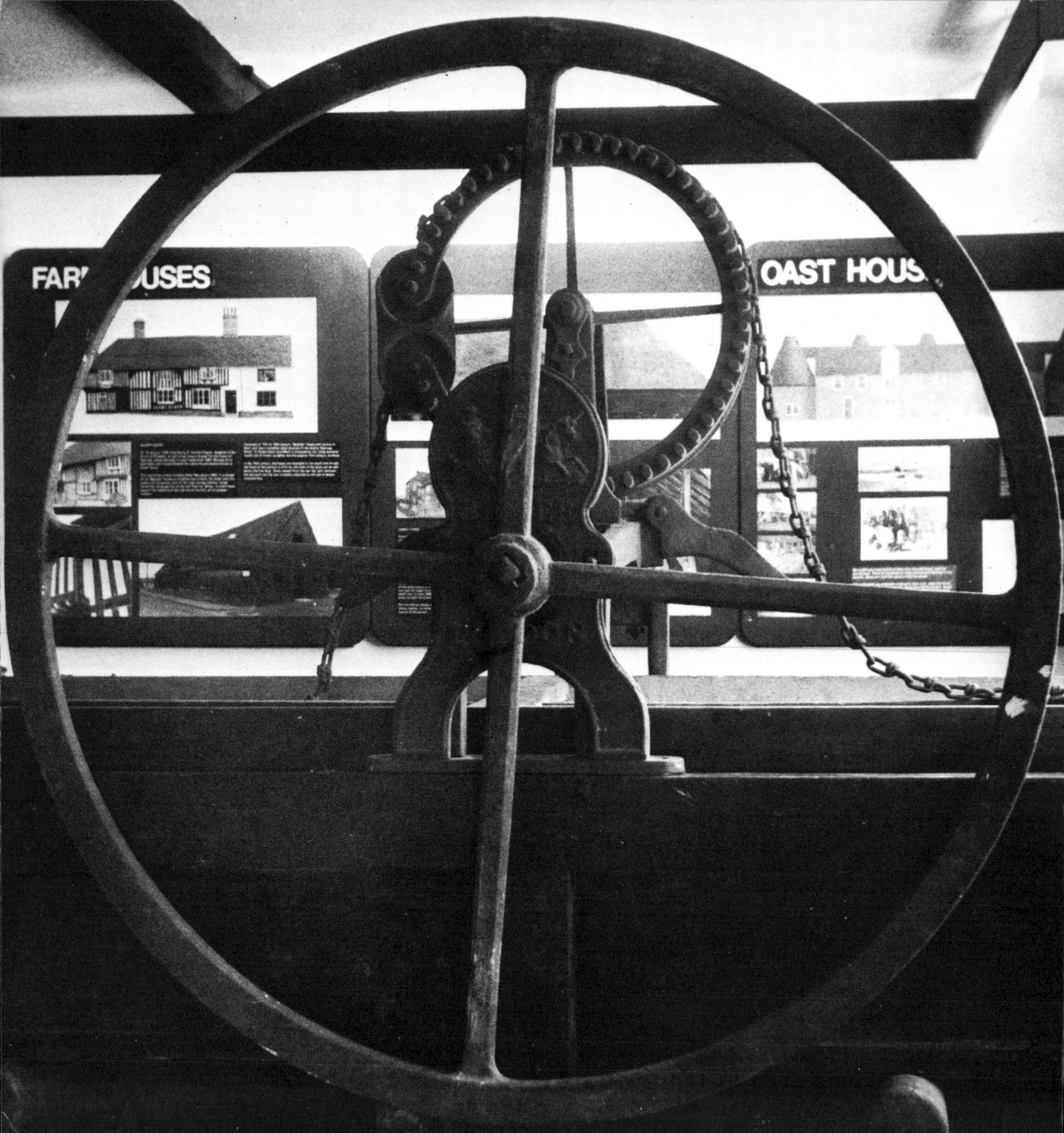

FARM HOUSES
OAST HOUS

Principles of Urban Interpretation

Everything that man has made has a voice. Every earth bank, every wall of baked brick or cut stone, every iron beam speaks of the men who made them, telling us much, not only about the secrets of their technique, but about the thought and the aspiration which led them to apply that technique in the way they did . . .

But before we can read this language we need knowledge and mental discipline to steer a right course between the opposite poles of the two cardinal errors that can sway our judgement: the error of hindsight which, by the application of our own standards to the work of the past, leads to contempt; and the romantic error which regards the past as a golden age and looks upon all its work with uncritical admiration.

L T C Rolt, *Navigable Waterways, 1969*

An urban interpretation scheme should not be seen as just another excuse for a nostalgic view of a rose-tinted past, or a virtuoso display of abstruse local knowledge. Its message should be fivefold:

— *No-one can plan properly for the future without understanding the past and the present.*

— *Most communities are far richer in architectural and historic interest than is usually supposed–particularly by those who live there and often even by those who think they know them well.*

— *The nation's story is easier to bring to life if it can be seen reflected in local events, changes and trends; and conversely that the urban fabric can throw telling light on the nation's social, economic, cultural and political evolution.*

— *Structures from the past, including the recent past, are a particularly effective means of giving present and future generations a better understanding of their forbears, the society in which they lived, and their material and spiritual aspirations.*

— *Once people have a better insight into the character of their own communities they are better equipped to intervene, as is their right, and perhaps their duty, when they sense a risk of some environmental blunder; and, just as important, to play their own constructive part in improving what needs to be improved in their surroundings.*

To bring this message home a variety of media is available— from town trails to heritage centres—but the first stage in any urban interpretation scheme is not to decide which to use. There are two others which come first, and eight in all:

(1) STOCKTAKING The first stage is to undertake a methodical assessment of resources—in other words to look hard at the community's fabric to see what it reveals about its development, how it reflects the story of the nation, what individual qualities it has, and where it has environmental characteristics (good or bad) from which lessons may be learnt for the future—or elsewhere.

(2) OBJECTIVES Next, possible objectives have to be identified. Is the aim to stimulate interest in a whole community, for example, or to forcus attention on one under-rated area or forgotten asset? And *whose* interest is it desired to stimulate—residents', visitors', officials', children's or some combination of these? In many communities several distinct objectives are likely to emerge.

(3) MEDIA Interpretation can be on a person-to-person or person-to-group basis, for example when a group of visitors is conducted round an area of interest by someone who knows a lot about it. There is no doubt that this can be rewarding for both parties, but unless means (or knowledgeable volunteers) are unlimited, this is the least flexible interpretive medium for it can operate only when both parties have time to meet. Less rigid are media which rely on display, printed or recorded material. So now comes the time to decide which medium to

harness to each objective—to tailor the means to the end. A published wall-sheet may look like the best way of developing appreciation of an under-rated area, a pair of trails of stimulating new interest in the fabric of a whole community.

(4) STRATEGY If it emerges that there is scope for several interpretive ventures, an overall strategy should be drawn up. As well as taking into account any urgent priorities and resources of manpower and cash, this should allow for facilities which are co-ordinated with one another.

(5) MONEY-RAISING In financial terms the strategy may be based not only on money in the bank but on what can reasonably be expected to accrue by way of grants and/or money-raising efforts. An early start needs to be made on exploring the first source of cash and exploiting the second.

(6) RESEARCH Meanwhile research should be under way. The first, stocktaking, stage will have thrown up dozens of questions to which answers have never been sought before. Given for example that there is an enclave of stone-built dwellings in a community where otherwise brick reigns supreme, what is the explanation? Was it a developer's whim, a requirement of a landlord's ground-lease, or something to do with the fact that the opening of a new railway or canal had made stone temporarily cheaper than brick?

(7) IMPLEMENTATION With research and money-raising complete, work can start on the creation of the interpretive material. What this involves will depend on the medium selected. Writers, artists and designers will be busy at all events and if the project is big they will need written briefs.

(8) PUBLICITY Some interpretive media—outdoor display boards and cases for example—will need little publicity for, once in position, they are there for all to see. However in other cases, such as those of trails and conservation area guides, publicity will be needed to bring them to the public's notice. This has to be repeated, not of the once-for-all variety.

These are but brief outlines of each stage and more is said about all of them on pp 19–60. But some basic principles need stating first. Put baldly, these are that to be successful an interpretive project must:

  (a) **Focus the senses**
  (b) **Tell the truth**
  (c) **Look for immediate links with the past**
  (d) **Bear the user's need in mind**
  (e) **Stimulate thought and further exploration**

Common sense? The implications are still worth spelling out.

(a) Focus the senses

Ask an environmentalist why interpretation is so important and almost certainly the reply will be 'It makes people use their eyes'. Quite right.

In the past too many mistakes have been made (often with the best of intentions) simply because people had not used their eyes. It was only after the felling of a key tree that everyone realised it had been an essential feature of a well-loved scene; after the demolition of an 'ordinary' cottage that everyone recognised it as the last, important example of its kind in the area; after the construction of the new warehouse astride the old branch line that everyone regretted the blocking of what could have become a useful traffic-free route for pedestrians, and might one day be needed as a railway again. The tree, or the cottage, or the branch line could have figured in a town trail or some other interpretive medium; even if none of them did, the chances are that if a programme of interpretation had increased public awareness generally the mistakes would not have been made.

However it is not just a question of opening people's eyes. As well as sight we have four other senses. Each can contribute to understanding, and often enjoyment; interpretation should try to bring them all into play.

A brewery (or a tannery!) can be scented long before it is seen; so too can some species of tree. The whine of a saw can betray a timber yard before it is within sight. In parts of England a gentle tap on a brick wall yields a disconcertingly hollow sound—revealing that it is not built of bricks at all, but has a hollow timber frame hung with mathematical tiles made to resemble bricks. *There* lies a story, too—partly of 18th-century owners who wanted to give their 16th-century homes an up-to-date brick look; partly of a hard-pressed Government seeking to raise money by a tax on bricks, and of resourceful builders legally evading it by using mathematical tiles instead.

When they first touch old oak beams, many people are still surprised to find the wood, worm-eaten though it may be, nearly as hard as iron. The first clue to the site of an old water-mill may be the sound of water rushing over a disused weir. Less picturesquely the strident noise of lorries may explain why so many homes along a particular road are equipped with double-glazing—paradoxically at the owners' expense, not the hauliers'. In the sense that local drinks, dishes or delicacies are part of a community's distinctive character, even taste can be brought into play. More than this, there are some foods (fish is the best example) that have helped fashion a settlement's economy, development and—sometimes—appearance.

So a fundamental principle of urban interpretation is that people should be encouraged to use not only their eyes but all five senses.

(b) Tell the Truth

A second principle, equally fundamental, is that as far as is humanly possible people should be told the truth and nothing but the truth. The *whole* truth they cannot be told in the space available: it must be distilled to provide the essence, and herein lies the danger of involuntary bias. Different ages, different nationalities, different classes will tend to extract different truths from the same facts, the same events, the same site and associations. So interpretation should be undertaken with a certain humility, in the knowledge that one is striving for an objectivity which can never be absolute.

A punctilious regard for accuracy must inform every stage. Interpreters have always been susceptible to the twin temptations of embroidery and suppression. Traditionally those most vulnerable are the custodians of certain historic buildings. Over the years the content and timing of their patter has been refined to a degree which would do credit to a top-rank television comic. Unfortunately its accuracy is no match for its entertainment value and the visitor departs ill-informed and misinformed.

Some local historians who ought to know better are just as bad—a rumour or theory becomes a tradition, and in no time a tradition becomes a fact. At the same time even if, for example, a quick glance at a building is sufficient to make clear to many people that it was built, or rebuilt, a hundred years after 'Queen Elizabeth slept here', the information is suppressed. As a result anyone, child or adult, just beginning to grasp the succession of regional building styles is confused; and anyone already conversant with this is likely to question the authenticity of every subsequent statement by the same writer.

(c) Look for immediate links with the past

To argue in this kind of case that the statement is 'virtually true' because Queen Elizabeth certainly slept in the house *on the site* only suggests a failure to understand another key principle of urban interpretation—that by far the most useful links with the past are the tangible ones. In terms of immediacy, the house where a famous figure once lived, revealing a good deal about his means, taste and lifestyle, is a prince compared with the pauper of a sad plaque on a modern office block recording that so-and-such a composer 'lived in a house on this site'. Informed imagination can run riot on the one but never get off the mark on the other.

This kind of historical association may seem the most colourful but others, generic rather than specific, reveal more about our forbears' everyday life. Buildings and other urban features reflect the uses for which they were designed and the kind of society which prevailed at the time. They are a form of documentary evidence as valid and immediate as any manuscript, and interpretation can highlight the clues they afford. Two or three examples illustrate the point.

Not everyone may realise that in middle-class town houses of the 18th and 19th centuries servants spent most of their lives in basements and attics. Those who do may not realise until it is pointed out by reference to particular examples just how ill-lit and ill-ventilated many basements were—and how for that matter unheated, uninsulated attics bore the brunt of winter cold and summer heat.

Even into the 20th century many town streets were surfaced only with loose gravel, with the result that in winter they were muddy and in summer (despite the ministrations of the water-cart) dusty. At key intersections and elsewhere where pedestrian traffic was heavy crossings were therefore laid in setts, and some of these can still be seen. A self-employed, self-appointed crossing-sweeper kept the setts clean and made a kind of a living out ot the tips he recieved from users. For pedestrians who got their feet muddy nonetheless, boot-scrapers were installed outside the front door—often built-in alongside it. In most towns hundreds or thousands of these still survive, but mostly unnoticed because they are at ground level. The countless different patterns—some plain, some florid, some Gothic, some classical—reveal a good deal about changing 19th century taste.

(d) Bear the user's needs in mind

To bear the user's needs in mind seems obvious enough. And yet . . .? Here, to illustrate some of the pitfalls, is a brief extract from a fictitious town trail:

> Past the next turning is Keeley Lodge, named after the well-known actor, and still a private house. Built of Hornton stone, it is a notable for its caryatids. It was built in the days of the window tax, as can be seen. The monkey-puzzle tree in the grounds is said to have been planted in 1864 by a member of the Royal Family. From beneath it a good view can be obtained of the famous spire of Listerton Church, which as a matter of interest is in the next county.

As a piece of descriptive prose, this seems unexceptionable. As interpretation, it is a disastrous failure. The average user who is new to the area will be baffled.

First he will have to find out for himself whether 'the next turning' is on the right or left, and whether it is 50 or 500 yards further on.

When he reaches Keeley Lodge he will find that its grounds are so ample that the main front is hidden by trees and that he can look at it only by walking up a gravel drive. If the owners are in and notice him gazing at the house they may mistake him for a burglar 'casing the joint' and call the police.

If they are out he may begin by speculating why the house is named after Keeley. Was it built for him, perhaps, or just for an admirer? Come to think of it, who *was* Keeley? Well-known in the area, evidently, and perhaps in his day, but *un*known to most people today.

Hornton stone: well, yes; it is a striking ochre colour—but why is that, where does it come from, and is there anything else special about it? Perhaps there are traces of iron—that would explain the colour. But there is nothing about it in the trail.

Caryatids? Caryatids? What are they—those elaborate chimneys, the stone urns along the balustrade, or those strange draped figures supporting the entrance porch roof? Never mind, let's have a look at the windows. Ah yes, some *are* blocked up. Everyone knows about the window tax. But when was it? It would help to date the building after all!

Now where's this monkey-puzzle tree? It doesn't say which member of the Royal Family planted it, or why. No sign of it in front—it must be round the back. Can't very well go there, so I can't see the view. Perhaps sometimes the grounds are open to the public, but it doesn't say so here. Can't say I've ever heard of Listerton Church anyway. What's so famous about its spire? It doesn't say here. In the next county, is it? Well here that could be one of several and in any case I don't see anything very interesting about it. Why did I ever start this wild goose chase?

So . . . there are plenty of pitfalls. How can they be avoided? It helps to bear in mind some simple rules:

— On a trail *always give clear directions.*

— *Do not draw attention to buildings which cannot be seen from a public highway or footpath*—unless they are open to the public, in which case state *when* they are open.

— *Never credit users with more knowledge than they are likely to possess.* The acid test with figures like Keeley is to ask people outside the area and without any knowledge of the particular profession whether they have ever heard of him. If they have not, and he has some significant association with the building in question, say who he was and explain the association.

— *Never use technical terms without explaining them.* Some, but probably not all, local people will know what are the characteristics of Hornton stone and where it is quarried; whilst most people would be unable to describe a caryatid. Explanation may be by way of parenthesis, a glossary or illustration, according to the medium. It is not just a question of *definition*: the characteristics of a local stone will have dictated the form and appearance of buildings where it is used; while caryatids betoken architects' and patrons' revived interest in classical antiquities.

— *Never miss an opportunity of putting local events, changes or trends in their national context.* Of the window tax it would have been helpful to say that it was introduced in 1695 (during a reform of Government finances) and abolished in 1851 (during another); possibly also that as the brunt of taxation during the period was designed to fall on the better-off, cottage property was exempt. If the visible legacy of the tax is specially evident in the area as a whole, even more could be said.

— *If a feature is highlighted always give a clear indication of its date and identify any interesting characteristics.* It may seem unnecessary to say this but in fact the example of Keeley House makes clear that it is: its date is not given and though in all likelihood, as a biggish 18th or early 19th century house standing in its own grounds, it is a handsome, well-detailed building, no commentary on it is offered.

— *Never patronise users.* This is another way of saying that a fine balance has to be struck between crediting them with more knowledge than they are likely to possess (see above) and crediting them with less. Superfluous information, as well as irritating the user, also wastes space—and therefore money. But when a term does require explanation because many people will be unfamiliar with it, the trick may be to give the impression that of course the particular user is not one of them.

— *Test-use is essential before completion.* While it is still in draft the interpretive material should be shown to an interested outsider. However much care has been taken, the chances are that this will reveal mistakes, obscurities or missed opportunities.

— *Do not concentrate on the past to the exclusion of the present.* Residents, let alone visitors, often know little about what goes on behind the factory gates or the office swing-doors, yet it is employment of one kind and another which provides most communities with their economic base. Even in a small town the range of manufactured products can be surprisingly large and quite often a small firm in insignificant premises is producing commodities or components which are essential to the success of some larger business or enterprise. In economic and social terms such service facilities as hotels, hospitals, bus stations and transport depots are also significant. The work done in offices should not be overlooked, either. Many large concerns have de-centralised their HQs so that important functions are carried out in sateliete offices, while sometimes architectural or other professional practices with a national or international reputation are based in quite small communities. Most co-operative societies, many building societies and some trade unions and insurance companies have head offices outside the big conurbations.

(e) Stimulate thought and further exploration

Interpretation fails if all it supplies is information about particular features in isolation from their wider physical and historical contexts, if all it prompts is single-minded admiration for one particular buliding or area. Panegyric can be daunting, even damaging, if it carries with it the implication that other areas have nothing in common with the one being interpreted, or do not bear comparison with it. Certainly attractive features should be pinpointed and described, but what *makes* them attractive should also be pointed out. There may, after all, be a moral which can be applied elsewhere. The outsider may then on returning to his own area recognise for the first time that it possesses similiar qualities, or, given a bit of adroit attention, could do so.

It goes without saying that interpretation should encourage further exploration of the subject-area itself. If there are other interpretive facilities they should be referred to. Otherwise, a word or two in the right place is all that is needed to steer users into the side-streets to make their own discoveries.

Some trails (particularly those designed for children) include a kind of quiz, pointing out that certain buildings have interesting features and inviting users to identify and/or explain them. A questionnaire of this kind can be quite instructive for adults, too, if they accompany their children. Rather more sophisticated is the consumer response approach. Users are invited to complete a questionnaire giving their impressions of an area and return it to the organisation responsible for the interpretive initiative. Apart from the fact that this yields genuinely useful information, it seldom fails to stimulate users to ferret around for themselves.

In most places, too, there will be plenty of scope for a cautionary element. Where interpreters are confident in their judgement there is no reason why they should not point out solecisms—the way in which the use of artificial stone-cladding or the insertion of modern windows has wrecked the character and proportions of a Victorian house, for example. If there is frankness about one community's blunders, it may help others to avoid them. Is the High Street full of empty shops and is the explanation that the local council was lured by the treacherous bait of a higher rateable base into doing a deal with a property company for a new 'shopping centre' nearby? Is the reason for a particular street looking down-at-heel that it is blighted by road proposals which everyone except an obstinate highway authority now recognises as being an expensive and damaging luxury? If so, say so, but not in any querulous spirit—a laconic approach may even be most effective.

For the most part, though, interpretation is probably at its most stimulating when it pinpoints and analyses those urban qualities which though undeniably attractive have often defied analysis before. One example is the old building, wholly devoid of architectural polish, which still has charm. Why? It has evolved organically over the centuries, alterations and additions having been sympathetically undertaken in local materials to produce a harmonious whole. Another is the irregular space—site of a forgotten market, perhaps?—at the heart of a village. Five streets converge here, but not as a 20th-century highway engineer would design them. The junction, and the space, have evolved over centuries to meet the needs of villagers, traders, even perhaps friars and evangelists. It is a comfortable place, still the focal point where people come to gossip. Underfoot, still stone setts in the centre, York slabs along the sidewalks, and Guernsey granite kerbs at the edges. Subtle textures, grains, tones and colours are the established complement to those of the buildings around. There are lessons here, surely for elsewhere.

Stages in an Interpretive Programme

'Ay, the toppermost class nowadays have left off the use of wheels for the good of their constitutions, so they traipse and walk for many years up foreign hills, where you can see nothing but snow and fog, till there's no more left to walk up; and if they reach home alive, and ha'n't got too old and weared out, they walk and see a little of their own parishes.

So they tower about with a pack and a stick and a clane white pocket-handkerchief over their hats just as you see he's got on his. He's been staying here a night, and is off now again. "Young man, young man," I think to myself, "if your shoulders were bent like a bandy and your knees bowed out as mine be, till there is not an inch of straight bone or gristle in 'ee, th' wouldstn't go doing hard work for play 'a b'lieve." '

Thomas Hardy, *The Hand of Ethelberta, 1876*

With these general principles in mind, further thought can be given to the stages involved in any interpretive project.

(1) STOCKTAKING

The object of this, as already stated, must be to look hard at the community's fabric to see what it reveals about its development, how it reflects the story of the nation, what individual qualities it has, and where it has environmental characteristics (good or bad) from which lessons may be learnt for the future—or elsewhere.

For those already knowledgeable about the area there is often a strong temptation to omit this process—but it should be avoided. Unless it is undertaken the danger is that interpretation will focus on the most obvious features of interest, to the detriment of others less conspicuous but no less significant—for example the way in which settlement patterns have been influenced by natural features; the way key buildings such as abbeys, market houses and factories have helped to shape street patterns; vernacular building characteristics; floorscapes and rooflines; and building details which are interesting for their craftsmanship, innovative qualities, or the insight they afford into social history.

It helps if the stocktaking can take the form of a methodical *search* for features which highlight a community's physical setting and link it with events, trends and changes important in the nation's development. A check list (in rough chronological order and by no means exhaustive) of such features is printed as Appendix 1 (p 109) and it may be a good idea to photocopy this, tick those which can be seen locally, and add any others not included.

A particularly good idea is to invite an outsider or two to help with the appraisal. They seldom fail to notice points of interest overlooked by local people. The changing design of shops, it may be, or the way in which one outlying settlement along the main road was developed ahead of its time because the old pub at its heart was made a terminus for horse buses or trams. If one outsider wants to know the explanation, others will too.

Remember too that though in one area ordinary grey bricks, millstone grit or pantiles will seem perfectly ordinary because they are the common coinage of building in the locality, they may seem unusual, and therefore interesting, to a visitor from Cornwall or the Cotswolds, where materials are very different.

Industrial buildings old and new, should never be overlooked. Whatever their architectural interest, all will afford clues to the growth (or in some cases decline) of a place. Locally a warehouse or a woollen mill may not seem a very noteworthy feature but for some visitors it may be the most arresting feature in the area. They will want to know why it is where it is and how it relates (say) to a railway, canal, river or nearby buildings. Its form and appearance will have been dictated by the production techniques prevailing at the period—whether dependent (as they were in the 19th century) for a score of benches to take their drive direct from a common shaft or (as they often are today) on electricity to provide independent power. Was there ever a major strike which throws light on the nation's social and political development, or a disaster which illustrates progress in industrial safety?

It is particularly important to avoid the 'history-stops-at-1830' (or even 1930) syndrome. It is not only that many 19th and 20th century buildings are attractive in design and/or craftsmanship but that they reveal just as much about social, economic and cultural developments as their predecessors—and after all these developments have been more rapid and far-reaching in the last 150 years than ever before.

Thus almost every town has at least one area of 'bye-law' housing—terraces of dwellings built after the Public Health Act of 1875. This might be regarded as the first planning legislation in Britain since it gave local authorities powers not only to control sanitary conditions in towns but also to regulate the construction of new housing and the dimensions of new streets. It had the effect of raising housing standards, of ensuring that enough space was left between buildings for adequate light and air, and of seeing that houses were structurally sound; but the second requirement also encouraged developers to build properties in row upon row of monotonous terraces. Streets of this kind are documentary evidence of a major Victorian effort to tackle the problem of the slums, and testimony indirectly to the fear of slum-generated epidemics which stimulated the effort.

Today few close-packed jerry-built slums of the Victorian kind survive, but there are still pockets of sub-standard housing. Sometimes under General Improvement Area or Housing Action Area procedures the existing properties and their environment are improved— and examples are worth pointing out. Sometimes on the other hand housing authorities consider clearance the only option. It may be worth drawing attention to the area threatened with clearance, perhaps comparing it with one nearby which is being improved, and asking whether it might not be better to rehabilitate both.

Invaluable as a reference tool in the stocktaking process if the manpower is available to start compiling it is a Dictionary of Local Biography— a local counterpart of the familiar DNB. If DLBs were generally available the work of historians as well as interpreters would be much easier. Few, if any, exist, but the difficulty lies more in making a start than in maintaining effort. In a voluntary organisation the task may appeal particularly to someone with an interest in local history.

Equally useful if the time can be found to compile it is a basic handbook of local facts and figures, past and present. In interpretive work these will be needed time and again, but many of them will prove surprisingly elusive. It is a good idea to draw up a check-list of basic questions to which it would be useful to have answers readily available. Some will refer to the past and can be answered once and for all; some will refer to the present and will require systematic updating. All details should be properly referenced, of course. The result will be a permanent reservoir of information which can be easily consulted. There may even be a case for publishing it in its own right, say as 'Forchester Facts and Figures 1066–1979', with perhaps a new edition every five years. Some information of this kind used to be included in national gazetteers and county directories, but these are now produced only in more perfunctory form; some of it likewise (but usually only the barest minimum) is often included in those 'Official Guides' whose main concern seems to be to attract industrialists and residents. Therefore there ought to be a market for local handbooks of this kind, even if for reasons of economy they are only duplicated.

The value of the finished handbook (whether in manuscript or published form) will be a function of the amount of thought given to the checklist of questions. One of the best lists* of the kind was drawn up nearly 200 years ago in connection with a publisher's plans to issue a series of books on British topography. It can be elaborated to take into account the many changes which have taken place since but most of the questions are still as pertinent as ever. It is reprinted here partly because of this and partly because it serves to highlight topics that are still relevant but can all too easily be overlooked.

---

*The list of Queries, published in 1780 by John Nichols as part of Bibliotheca Topographica Britannica No 1, was based on several earlier, but shorter questionnaires (as we should now call them) of the same kind. Printer, author and patron of topographical scholarship, Nichols (1745–1826) can now be seen almost as a pioneer of interpretation. 'As there is no science which is not capable of being facilitated by general rules,' he wrote in the 'Advertisement' to the Queries, 'that of Antiquity, so far as it relates to the illustration of our national Topography and History, . . . may . . . be forwarded, by suggesting even to the most incurious observer subjects worthy his notice, and the communication of which to others may yield the double benefit of instruction, both to the antiquary and the citizen.'

Queries *proposed to the* Nobility, Gentlemen, Clergy, *and
others, of* Great Britain *and* Ireland ;
*With a view of obtaining, from their Answers respecting the Places
of their Residence, a more perfect Account of the Antiquities and
Natural History of those Kingdoms than has yet appeared.*

The Answers to be addressed to the Editor of the Bibliotheca
Topographica Britannica, *to the Care of* J. Nichols, *Printer,*
Red-Lion-Passage, Fleet-Street, post paid.

1. WHAT is the antient and modern name of the parish,
and its etymology ?

2. What is its distance from the hundred town, county town,
or next market town ?

3. By what parishes is it bounded, E. W. N. and S.? and what
are its length and breadth ?

4. What distance is it from London and the chief towns
round, and what is the price of carriage per hundred weight ?

5. What is the extent of the parish ?

6. What number of hamlets, villages, townships, chapelries,
inn-ships, districts, wards, are in it? their names and situation?
and to what division, hundred, liberty, or constabulary belonging ?

7. What are the number of its houses and inhabitants of every
kind, and of its teams? List of freeholds and copyholds, and
their holders ?

8. What number of persons have been married, christened,
and buried, for the space of 20 years last past, compared with the
first 20 years of the register? When did the register begin?
Are any curious remarks made therein?

9. What manors are or were in it, and who are or were
lords thereof ?

10. What are the names and qualities, arms and descent, of
their proprietors ?

b

11. Are

11. Are there any particular cuftoms or privileges, or remarkable tenures, in any of the manors in the parifh? What courts, and their cuftoms? What exempt jurifdictions civil or ecclefiaftical?

12. What caftle, fort, ancient manor or manfion houfe, feat, villa, or other remarkable buildings, are or have been in the parifh? and the dimenfions of their largeft apartments or galleries?

13. What coats of arms, infcriptions, dates, or other ornaments and figures, are or were carved or painted in and about any of their buildings?

15. In what manor, diocefe, deanry, and hundred, does the CHURCH ftand?

16. Is it dedicated to any faint? When and by whom was it built, of what materials, and has it a tower or fpire?

18. What are its dimenfions, number of ailes, chapels, and bells?

19. Are there any ancient or modern monuments, graveftones, or brafs plates? and what infcriptions and arms in the church, chancel, or fteeple, or on the bells, plate, chefts, pews, fcreens, &c. or, in the church-yard? Are the font, altar-piece, or plate, remarkable? Or, are there any other remains of antiquity?

20. Are there any painted figures, arms, or infcriptions, in the windows?

21. Are there any tables of benefactions, or other infcriptions which are worthy notice, painted or carved in or about the church, within or without? or any parochial library in the church or parfonage?

22. What chantries, altars, fhrines, lights, images, gilds, or roods, appear to have been in the church; or what privileges and indulgencies annext to it? What reliques, miracles, and legends?

23. Are there any vaults or burial-places peculiar to any ancient or other families? and what extraordinary interments or prefervation of bodies?

24. Is

24. Is the living a rectory, vicarage, donative, or finecure?

25. Are the computed worth of the living and its rate in the King's books rightly stated in Ecton's Thefaurus?

26. Who are, or have been, patrons?

27. Who are, or have been, incumbents as far back as you can trace? and were any of them remarkable for their writings, fufferings, or other particulars? of what univerfity or college, what their degrees and preferments, and where buried?

28. Are there any lands belonging to the glebe or vicarage, or any copy of the endowment, or any terrier? Has it been augmented by queen Anne's bounty? What are the firft-fruits, tenths, fynodals, procurations and penfions paid out of the profits?

29. Who is poffeffed of the great tithes? what may their reputed value be? and is any modus paid thereout, and to whom?

30. Is there any chapel of eafe in the parifh? how is it fupported? and who are, or have been, incumbents? and of what value may the cure be fuppofed?

31. What charities or benefactions belong to the parifh? when and by whom given? how improved, or how loft?

32. Are there any Diffenting or other meeting-houfes, or Popifh chapels? and what number of each perfuafion may be in the parifh?

33. Are there any colleges, alms-houfes, free or other fchool, or hofpital; by whom and when founded, for how many objects, and whether abufed or loft; or the prefent ftate?

34. Have there been any abbies, priories, friaries, nunneries, hermitages, fanctuaries, or other religious houfes; or are there any remains or ruins of them? by whom founded, and to whom granted? what charters, cartularies, ledger-books, rentals, ftatutes, deeds, wills, obituaries, bede-rolls, or other writings, feals, habits, fhrines, or other fragments, belonging to any church, monaftery, chantry, gild, hofpital, fchool, or other charity?

35. Are there any croffes or obelifks, infcribed or carved ftones, circles of rude ftones, fingle ftones on hillocks, or otherwife,

wife, hollows wrought into rocks, single stones placed horizontally or over one another, or any beacons, in the parish?

36. Are there any barrows or tumuli, or extraordinary mounts? have any been opened, and what has been found therein?

37. Are there any *Roman, Saxon,* or *Danish* castles, forts, camps, roads, ditches, banks, pits, or other extraordinary earth-works, or pieces of antiquity remaining in your parish; and what traditions or historical accounts are there of them?

38. Have there been any vaults, pavements, urns, pieces of pottery, lamps, weapons, armour, seals, rings, buckles, odd pieces of metal, statues, busts, carvings, altars, images, coins, or other pieces of antiquity, *Roman, Saxon, Danish*, or other, or bones of extraordinary size, dug up in your parish; when and by whom; and in whose custody are or were they?

39. Have there been any remarkable battles fought, on what spot, by whom, when, and what traditions are there relating thereto? or what the sufferings or adventures of the clergy or gentry in the civil wars?

40. Have any councils, synods, parliaments, or other meetings, civil or religious, been held in it?

41. Have you any wake, Whitsun ale, doles, or other such customs, used in the parish; or any annual or other processions or perambulations?

42. What markets or fairs are kept in the parish; what commodities are chiefly brought for sale; are they the manu-factures or produce of the country, live cattle, or other things; what toll is paid, and to whom?

43. Is there any statute fair for hiring of servants, and how long has it been established? What are the usual wages for men and maid servants, &c. for each branch of husbandry?

44. Are there any manufactures carried on in the parish, and what number of hands are employed? What rare pieces of art have been invented or made by any of the parishioners?

45. What

45. What is generally a day's wages for labourers in hufbandry and other work; and what for carpenters, bricklayers, mafons, or other mechanics, &c.?

46. What are, or have been, the prices of provifions, beef, veal, mutton, lamb, pork, pigs, geefe, ducks, chicken, rabbits, butter, cheefe, &c.?

47. What is the annual rent or value of the lands or houfes in the parifh, or townfhip? what is the poor's rate in the pound *communibus annis*? and how much land-tax is paid at 4s. in the pound?

48. What common, or quantity of wafte land, may be in the parifh?

49. Are there any forefts, chaces, parks, or warrens; of what extent, number of deer, &c.? any heronries, decoys, or fifheries?

50. What is the ufual fuel? is it coal, wood, heath, furze, turf, or peat? and the prices paid on the fpot?

51. Is there any great road leading through the parifh, and from noted places?

52. Do any rivers, or brooks, or navigable canals, rife in or run through the parifh? when and on what terms were the acts for making them navigable obtained? what fort of boats are ufed on them, and what is the price of carriage per hundred or ton to your parifh?

53. What bridges, when, and by whom built, of what materials, what number of piers or arches, the length and breadth of the bridge, and width of the arches? are they fupported by private or public coft?

54. Has the parifh given birth or burial to any man eminent for learning, or other remarkable or valuable qualifications?

55. What particular games, fports, cuftoms, proverbs, or peculiar words or phrafes, or names of places, perfons, animals, vegetables, or things, are ufed; and what notions or traditions obtain among the common people?

56. Are

56. Are there, in any of the gentlemen's or other houses, any pictures which give infight into any hiftorical facts, or any portraits of men eminent in art, fcience, or literature; any ftatues, bufos, or other memorial, which will give any light to paft tranfactions? or what manufcripts in any language, books of arms, pedigrees, lives, fignatures, patents, diplomas, perambulations, furveys, plans, pictures or drawings of any perfons, buildings or views relating to the parifh, in the poffeffion of any perfon in the parifh, or their acquaintance?

To thefe Queries if applied to *Cities, Market,* or *Corporate Towns,* may be added others refpecting their hiftory, foundations, ftreets, buildings, walls, gates, churches, wards, parifhes, charters, privileges, immunities, corporations, companies, gilds, government, and lift of mayors, fheriffs, recorders, reprefentatives, electors, bifhops, deans and other cathedral members; rates, taxes, trade, manufactures, fieges, accidents by fire, or otherwife.

QUERIES *relating to the* NATURAL HISTORY *of the* PARISH.

1. WHAT is the appearance of the country in the parifh; is it flat or hilly, rocky, or mountainous, open or inclofed; and the terms and mode of modern inclofing?

2. Do the lands confift of woods, arable, pafture, meadow, heath, or what?

3. Are they fenny or moorifh, boggy or firm, fertile or barren?

4. Is there fand, clay, chalk, ftone, gravel, loam, or what is the nature of the foil?

5. Have you any marble, moorftone, lime-ftone, free-ftone, ftone for building, coal, flate, pipe-clay, brick-clay? how is it got out, and how worked?

6. What minerals, falts, ochres, chalks, clays, marles, molds, earths, fands, gravels, flints, pebbles, &c. does the foil contain?

7. Is

7. Is there any marl, fullers earth, potters earth, or loam, or any other remarkable foils?

8. Are there any bitumen, naphtha, alum, calamine, black-lead, bifmuth, mercury, antimony, or other fubftances of that nature, found in the earth?

9. What ftrata of foil do they meet with on digging wells or other openings, and at what depth?

10. What petrifactions or foffils, either ftone or wood, are found in the parifh, and in what ftrata? Are there any figured ftones, fuch as echinitæ, belemnitæ, &c.; any having the impreffion of plants or fifh, or any foffil marine bodies, fuch as fhells, corals, &c. or any petrified parts of animals; any tranfparent pebbles, cryftallizations, or any fubftances otherwife remarkable; or foffil-trees, nuts, &c.?

11. Are there any mines? to whom do they belong, and what do they produce; their courfe and depth, the manner of working, and what obfervations have been made on them, or accidents by damps or otherwife? and what are the laws and cuftoms of thefe feveral mines?

12. How low do the fprings lye, and what fort of water do you meet with in the feveral parts of the parifh?

13. Are there any periodical fprings, which rife and fall, ebb and flow, and at what feafons, or bury themfelves under ground, or petrify and incruft, or produce any other extraordinary effects?

14. Are there any mineral fprings, frequented or not; at what feafons of the year reckoned beft, and what diftempers are they frequented for? What are their qualities, virtues, weight, and analyfis; and what cures attefted or wrought by them?

15. Are there any hot waters or wells for bathing, and for what diftempers frequented? any wells or ftreams formerly accounted holy?

16. Are there any lakes, meers, pools, or water-falls; what their depth and height; where do they rife, and whither do they run?

17. Are

17. Are there any subterraneous rivers, which appear in one place, then sink into the earth, and rise again?

18. Are there any mills on the rivers, and to what uses are they employed?

19. What is the proportion of arable, and meadow or pasture?

20. What are the chief produce of the lands, and in what proportion?

21. What is the general price paid for lands, arable, meadow, pasture, &c.

22. What sort of manure is chiefly used for the land, and what is the price of it on the spot?

23. What are the methods of tillage; what sorts of ploughs, and other instruments of husbandry are used; or have any new methods of cultivation been introduced?

24. What experiments have been made in agriculture, gardening, or the management of orchards, vineyards, hop-grounds, woods, or underwoods, cattle, poultry, bees, or fish-ponds?

25. Does the parish produce any quantities of timber, of what sort; and what are the prices on the spot per load or ton?

26. What trees thrive best, or are most common?

27. What plants, shrubs, grains, mosses, grasses, trees, fruits, flowers, are peculiar or most common? what uses are they applied to, and what their virtues?

28. Are there any and what quantities of saffron, woad, teazels, or other vegetables of that sort, growing in the parish; and what prices do they sell for on the spot?

29. Are there any hop or cherry gardens, or vineyards? and what is the price of their produce on the spot?

30. Are there any apple or pear orchards in the parish; what kind of cyder or perry is made, and at what sold for per hogshead on the spot?

31. Is the parish remarkable for breeding any cattle of remarkable qualities, colour, size, value, or number, and how sold; with other general observations?

32. Are

32. Are any quantities of sheep raised or fed in the parish; and on what do they chiefly feed?

33. What is the nature of the air; is it moist or dry, clear or foggy; healthy, or subject to produce agues, fevers, or other disorders; and at what time is it reckoned most so, and by what probable cause?

34. A register of weather and general state of the air for one year at least, kept by different persons, with incidental remarks, on the plan of " The Naturalists Journal," by the Hon. Daines Barrington.

35. What are the kinds of birds, insects, or reptiles, common or rare?

36. What sorts of fish do the rivers produce, what quantities, what are their prices on the spot, and in what seasons are they best?

37. What is the height of the mountains or hills, and what observations have been made on them?

38. Are there any remarkable caves or grottos, or other openings in the earth, natural or artificial?

39. Are the people of the country remarkable for make, size, strength, complexion, longevity, or any bodily or natural qualities? or have there been any exceptions to the general rules in their several cases?

40. What strange accidents, wonderful events, or extraordinary diseases and cures, have happened; or uncommon deaths, discoveries of murder, apparitions; what legends and traditions obtain about them, or what their attestation?

41. Is any part of the parish subject to inundations or land floods, or to be overwhelmed by torrents of sand, and their effects?

42. Hath there been any remarkable mischief done by thunder and lightning, storms, whirlwinds, or earthquakes?

43. Are there any remarkable echoes?

44. Have any remarkable phænomena or meteors been observed in the air?

c

If

If the Parish is on the SEA COAST.

45. Is the shore flat, sandy, high, or rocky, and the encroachment or returns of the sea on it?

46. What are the courses of the tides on the shore, or out at sea, the currents at a mile's distance, and other things worthy remark?

47. What kind of fish are caught there, in what quantity, at what prices sold, when most in season, how taken, and to what market sent?

48. What number of fishing vessels, of what sort, how navigated, and what number of hands are there in the parish?

49. How many ships, and of what burthen, belong to the parish?

50. What are the names of the creeks, bays, harbours, headlands, sands, rocks, or islands, near the coast?

51. What sea animals, plants, sponges, corals, shells, &c. are found on or near the coast?

52. Are any remarkable sea weeds used for manure, or curious on any other account?

53. Are there any remains of piers, camps, batteries, blockhouses, or other works, on the cliffs or shore; or any extraordinary caverns under them?

54. Have there been any remarkable battles or sea fights near the coast, any remarkable wrecks or accidents, which can give light to any historical facts?

55. What light-houses, or beacons?

STOCKTAKING—
FOR URBAN INTERPRETATION

Before any interpretive work is undertaken, a stocktaking of the local fabric should be carried out, to see what it reveals (*see pp 19–30 and the checklist of features of interest printed as Appendix 1, pp 109 – 114*).

To illustrate what opportunities may emerge, here is a selection of photographs taken in a fairly typical small town—Leek, in Staffordshire. With a population of just under 20,000, and a weekly retail market, Leek is an important local shopping centre, though some of the multiples have pulled out because it is 'too small'.

After centuries of quiet, organic development, the town grew rapidly in the 19th century with the intensification of the textile industry (which is still a force locally). This growth is reflected in the mill buildings themselves, contemporary housing, and much fine Victorian architecture in a varied range of styles.

In the past 90 years Leek's population has increased by only 50% (less than most towns') and because of this slow growth its centre has not fallen prey to the convulsions of redevelopment which have afflicted some other communities. But even in Leek there are unsightly crops of urban wasteland and dereliction.

Today the town's economic and social pattern is more complex than ever before, its business life more closely linked with the centre of the national stage. For in addition to the traditional textile industry, Leek plays host to the HQ of one of the biggest building societies, the HQ of a trade union, and a butter-packing factory with a national reputation. There is no passenger railway service (the nearest station is 12 miles away) but bus services radiate from the town and mass car-ownership has meant that many people live in Leek but work elsewhere (in the Potteries, for example)—or

THE IRREGULAR RECTANGLE where the *weekly market* is held has been the town's centre of gravity for centuries. Though the present-day *stalls* have metal frames, they look not unlike the wooden shambles which preceded them. But whereas 50 or 100 years ago most of the traders lived locally, today many of them come long distances in their vans. The buildings round the *Market Place* were designed to be a cut above the rest—taller, often bigger and more pretentious. Because buying and selling is thirsty work, there are *inns and pubs*, like 'The Cock', thus named no doubt because the facilities once included a *cockpit*. This particular inn has a special claim to fame, now recorded on a plaque *(inset):* it was here, on 21 April 1871, that the first steps were taken to found a *trade union*—the Amalgamated Society of Textile Workers and Kindred Trades. The local *silk industry* (probably introduced from Spitalfields in London via Derby) developed rapidly to cater for increasing demand in the 19th century. The union still has its HQ in Leek—in 'Foxlowe', a Georgian building within a few doors of 'The Cock' and seen here in the background. A private house until bought by the union in 1917, 'Foxlowe' takes its name from a nearby piece of land which belonged to the house's former owners. Like many other late 18th century buildings, the house relies for its handsome effect mainly on

BECAUSE PEOPLE like to feel that their money is secure, banks are usually solid and impressive-looking buildings. The *National Westminster Bank,* in the main street, meets these criteria without being dull. It was opened in 1883 as a branch of the Manchester and Liverpool District Banking Company Limited (later the District Bank), whose name still appears in the 'cartouche' over the entrance at the side. The *architects* were William Sugden and his son, W Larner Sugden, who between them were responsible for many other attractive buildings in the town.

The 19th century was a period when architects drew their inspiration mainly from the past, and the Sugdens were masters of several different styles. Here the style is eclectic (derived from more than one source), with the middle of the 17th century providing most of the inspiration. Dominant against the restraint of the rest of the building is the right-hand gable, with its pargetting (ornamental plasterwork) and elaborate windows based on 17th century work found in East Anglia and the South East. The tall chimneys serve as a foil to the building's horizontal emphasis.

The arms in the apex of the gable are those of the bank which built the premises and the Latin motto 'Decus Prudentiae Merces' suggests that 'distinction is the reward for careful money management'. The first banks were locally owned and had no branches, and at one time there were more than 600

individual firms in England. However today following a long series of *amalgamations* there are only four main banking groups in England. The District Bank was absorbed by the National Provincial Bank Ltd in 1962 and six years later this merged with the Westminster Bank Ltd to form the National Westminster Bank Ltd.

The building is well maintained by the owners and no unidiomatic alterations have been made to the facade. The main *sign* has been fitted in without detracting from the bank's appearance, while the projecting sign serves its purpose without being obtrusive. The use of a *'logo'* to denote 'corporate identity' became very popular in the 1960s and in its application of emblems revives a practice common when most people could not read or write.

THE CONCEPT of *education* for all is still quite a recent one in England—schooling was not made compulsory until 1870. But in most towns some effort was made before then to see that at least a few children gained a proper education. Often, as in Leek, the initiative was taken on a charitable basis and by someone who had left his home-town, made his fortune and wanted to give it a useful asset. Thomas Parker, Earl of Macclesfield (1666–1732), was the son of a Leek lawyer who found fame and fortune as Lord Chief Justice and Lord Chancellor, though later he fell into disgrace. In his late 50s he built this *Grammar School*, and his generosity is recorded in a contemporary (and elegantly carved) plaque on the front.

As in many other pre-19th-century schools, teaching took place on the upper floor, the ground floor being used as a romping place by the boys'.

Of course this small building would never have found room for all the children of Leek, nor was it intended to. All the endowment provided for was 'for teaching six poor boys of Leek to read', but the Master (headmaster) might take extra paying pupils to boost his salary. Schools such as this usually went on to teach Ancient Greek and Latin, since these were seen as essential foundations of knowledge and would be needed by those students who aspired to attend university. Science and modern languages had little place in the cur-riculum until the later 19th century but here in 1868 commer-cial subjects were being taught alongside Latin. By 1901 the school had closed, in effect superseded by others elsewhere in the town, and today the building serves as a *Scout Troop HQ*—an appropriate use which ensures its survival.

The tenacity of traditional building techniques and styles is well illustrated in the Grammar School. Built of *millstone grit* quarried locally, it is devoid of structural decoration and has simple mullioned windows (divided by vertical supports) which hark back to the 16th century. The style is virtually Pennine of the kind which prevailed in parts of Yorkshire, Lancashire, Staffordshire and Derbyshire for many years. The windows are latticed—provided with a mesh of glazing bars fine enough for very small panes of glass. By 1723 it was possible to obtain much larger panes. but perhaps small panes were used to save on replacement costs. Whatever the reason for their use, the diamond latticing adds a touch of lightness to what otherwise might seem a sombre building.

TO AN EXTENT this building wears its heart on its sleeve. It was presented in 1896, the plaque records, as the *Maude Church Institute,* 'for the use of the Parish Church of St Edward's, Leek, by a few parishioners as a memento of the Rev C B Maude's vicariate!

The 19th century saw a great revival in the *Church of England*. Churches (like St Edward's itself) were restored after centuries of neglect, congregations increased, and social activities developed—hence the need for new accommodation. Still used mainly for church purposes, the Maude Institute also houses a pre-school playgroup.

But the plaque tells only part of the story. In fact the building dates from 1843 and served as the *National School* for the Parish Church. A 'National School' was nothing to do with the Government: it was run under Church of England auspices on the principles of the National Society and provided elementary education for children whose parents could afford the very modest fees.

The building contrasts with its 1723 Grammar School neighbour in style—but not in scale, so that they harmonise with one another. In the century of the *Gothic revival,* there are such Gothic features as the hoods over the windows and the pointed entrance arch—but they smack more of playful 18th century 'Gothick' than the correct (but often duller) 19th century version.

MANY TOWNS had more than one *market place,* Beverley King's Lynn and Leek among them, but usually only one is left to serve its original purpose and it is only when a second market is perpetuated in a street name (as here in Leek) that its existence is readily recalled.

The building, now an office, was once a house. With its *ornamental canopy* over the entrance, it dates probably from the first half of the 18th century. Notice how the *windows* are set virtually flush with the facade.

Opening casements are built-in almost 'invisibly', without detracting from the visual unity of the whole window. The cast iron frames and glazing bars seem to be original and almost every pane is of original *'crown' glass*. Unlike 'sheet' glass (which has been in use since about 1832) crown glass has a slightly convex surface and each pane reflects a slightly different view. The charm of small crown glass panes has long been recognised by Christmas Card artists. In this particular case the variegated effect is intensified by the fact that the cast iron frames have become slightly bent. This is not due to any fault in manufacture, ageing, or settlement of the main fabric. It is because about 50 years ago their fireproof qualities were put sternly to the test when a milliner's shop opposite caught fire. They could not catch fire, but expansion under the intense heat did cause them to warp slightly.

ON THE FRINGE of the town centre, this street was built in the mid-19th-century to house some of the town's *growing population*. There are others like it, but each possesses its own individuality. House types are seldom precisely the same and quite small differences of detail can substantially alter the appearance of small properties such as these.

Here the *entrance arches,* with their fanlights, heak back to Georgian antecedents, though there are no elaborate door-cases. Most of the panelled *front doors* survive—and are likely to outlive the flimsy 'flush doors' sometimes substituted for them.

The *drainpipes* feed not into drains but into gulleys connecting with the street *gutter*—fine as long as the gulleys don't get blocked. There have always been stone setts in the gutters to carry off rainwater, but probably the *carriageway* originally had no more than a rough metalled surface.

Streets like this were well endowed with *small shops* and one can be seen in the foreground, though now converted into residential use. Such shops (with living accommodation behind and above) provided a modest livelihood when expected living standards were not as high as they are today. The *shopfront* is contemporary with the houses. With the elaborate wooden cornice, moulded pilasters, glazing bars, and crown glass, there is more than a lingering trace of

THIS GROUP of buildings' higgledy-piggledy appearance epitomises the old-established English town. An *array of building materials*—brick, tile, stone, slate, plaster and even roughcast—somehow combine to form a picturesque whole. The irregular *weathering* on the nearest house, however, suggests that it may need repair—and indeed it is empty at the moment.

The *raised plot* in front of the small white cottage suggests that at some time the road level was lowered—probably to ease the gradient along this steep stretch. This and the two nearest properties sport small *Georgian shopfronts*. Newest of the buildings is the three-storey one; it probably dates from about 1840 and now sells *antiques*.

These are all buildings old enough to have seen a good deal of change and adaptation. Just seen on the left projecting from an older house is a 1st floor bay window with mass-produced *stained glass* of the kind popular 70 or 80 years ago. At the entrance to Naylor Yard is a stumpy *bollard* intended to divert wayward wagon wheels which might otherwise have damaged the adjacent property. The cast-iron *street nameplate* has a robustness worthy of emulation today. The Parish Church's fine 14th-century *tower*, with its castellations and 19th-century pinnacles, dominates without overpowering the view. The Victorian *chimney-pots*, some spiky, some severe,

(2) OBJECTIVES

Forchester lies on the site of a minor Roman settlement where the main road from London to the north crosses the River Deven, which is navigable to a point just above the town. Well-sited for trade, Forchester came into early prominence as a market-town and has always been one of the largest communities in the county.

The ruins of the Norman castle form a prominent riverside feature and there are also remains of a Benedictine abbey and three other religious houses. Of the six medieval parish churches, four still survive. Religious free-thinking arrived early and the town is notable for its early meeting-houses, three of which remain in use and virtually unaltered. As several buildings still testify, it was an important coaching centre, and its strategic position was strengthened when it became an important junction first in the canal and then in the railway network. Today it is well served by two motorways, one cross-country and the other linking it with London and the north.

Until the late 18th century the town's main function was as a distribution centre but for the last 150 years its main importance has been as a centre of the engineering industry. Its position close to coalfields and iron-stone quarries allied to its good communications played a decisive role here.

Development of the local industry was mostly pioneered by the local families of Nicholson, Warrender and Oakes. Under their influence–and to a large extent out of their pockets–the town was largely re-shaped. Fine new public buildings, churches and chapels were erected, parks and walks laid out, and progressive municipal water, electricity and transport undertakings established. New housing development was notable for its spacious design, the Cliff area (overlooking the river) being especially notable in this respect. W. Vernon Heysham and Matthew Morris were two local architects whose work won them recognition well outside the town.

Today, with a population of 90,000, Forchester is a thriving community. New housing on the outskirts has enveloped without entirely submerging several old villages and thanks to the efforts of the borough council and local developers many of the town's older buildings have recently been given a new lease of life.

So, the gazetteer makes clear, Forchester (a fictitious place) is a fairly average medium-sized town. What kind of scope does it offer for interpretation, what might the objectives be? The stocktaking process will throw up a good many possibilities, not the least important of which would probably be to stimulate fuller appreciation of the town as a whole. However even if this ambitious objective is the one which in the end is given top priority it helps first to consider what some of the others might be. They may be divided into three categories—objectives related to a topical local issue; thematic objectives; and objectives designed to meet the needs of specific audiences, rather than a general one. It helps to draw up a list of the possibilities in each.

Issue-based objectives

(a) To focus attention on Forchester's *conservation areas* and the problems and opportunities within them. There are seven conservation areas in all (a point not mentioned in the gazetteer)—two in the town centre, one at the Cliff consisting mostly of large Victorian houses, and four in former village centres now within the borough boundary. In the two central areas the pace of rehabilitation has not been matched by the pace of environmental improvements (for example there is only one short pedestrian-priority street) and some upper floors are wasted. A plague of metal-framed windows has started to hit the Cliff area badly, and the old village centres, conversely, are falling victim to well-meaning but misdirected efforts to make silk purses out of sow's ears by the addition of spurious 'period' details to Victorian cottages.

(b) To focus attention on *derelict industrial sites* close to the town centre. The gazetteer is understandably reticent, but the harsh fact is that under the influence of the motorways several engineering firms have moved to new green-field sites, leaving derelict ones closer in. The historical and townscape importance of some of the abandoned buildings is considerable, and there has been a suggestion that one of them might house a regional museum of industrial archaeology. But the main need is for a purposeful communal approach to the redemption of the derelict areas.

(c) To highlight the qualities of *central area churches and chapels*. As industry has moved out, so has housing, and the congregations of town centre places of worship have dwindled almost to vanishing point. Already there is talk of de-roofing one of the medieval churches and leaving it a 'tidy ruin' while thought is being given to selling all three old meeting-houses for their site development potential.

Those who know the buildings recognise their architectural and townscape importance but some are down side-streets or in secluded courtyards and public apathy about their future is a function more of ignorance than of Philistinism.

(d) To re-assert *the advantages of a traditional shopping centre.* One of Forchester's strengths is that it has a pleasant High Street, with all the important multiples represented, and behind this a network of streets and yards where private traders, craftsmen and repair specialists flourish. However these facilities tend to be taken for granted and there are even plenty of unadventurous souls who have never explored the back-streets enough to know that oven-baked bread can still be bought there, spares obtained for the vacuum cleaner, or clocks repaired at modest cost. Forchester does not yet possess a modern multi-level shopping centre, but there is talk of one, and many of the smaller traders would be displaced by it, while the multiples would mostly abandon the High Street for it.

Thematic objectives

Even the gazetteer entry makes it clear that Forchester offers ample opportunities for straightforward, as opposed to issue-based, interpretation. The following are just a few of the themes it is possible to identify:

| Chronological |

Forchester's Roman Heritage/The Romans in Forchester
Medieval Forchester
Stuart Forchester
Georgian Forchester
Victorian Forchester
Forchester between the Wars
Post-War Forchester

| Topics |

Monastic Forchester
Worship in Forchester: *or sub-divide* . . .
  Forchester's Medieval Churches
  The Non-Conformists in Forchester
  Forchester and the Victorian revival
Transport for Forchester: *or sub-divide* . . .
  Coaching Forchester
  Forchester and the Railways
  Public transport in Forchester
  Forchester and the Motor Vehicle
Forchester goes to Market
Chimneys, Towers and Spires: Forchester's Skyline

Forchester's Yards and Courts
Industry in Forchester: *or sub-divide* . . .
  Forchester's Industrial Heritage/Forchester
    and the Industrial Revolution
  Working in Forchester Today
  Power for Forchester
Schooling in Forchester
Forchester Flora and Fauna
Forchester Philanthropists
Forchester's Pubs and Clubs
Law and Order in Forchester
Forchester Rejuvenated: The 19th Century Rebuilding
Sport in Forchester
Forchester Vernacular: Local Building Materials and Techniques
Two Victorian Architects: *or separately* . . .
  W Vernon Heysham and his Work
  Matthew Morris's Mark
Approaches to Forchester
Forchester's Listed Buildings/Forchester Conserved
All Mod Cons: Speculative Housing in Forchester

| Areas |

Waterside Forchester: *or sub-divide* . . .
  Along the Deven: Forchester's Quays and Trade
  Locks, Wharves, Warehouses and Tunnels: Canalside Forchester
Heart of Forchester
The Cliff
Forchester Villages: *or separately* . . .
  Davenford
  Burton Russell
  Thornhead
  Forringham

Audience-related objectives

There is also a third category of possible objectives—those related not to theme but to *audience*. Special provision may need to be made for such special groups as primary school children (who will derive only limited benefit from adult-orientated material) and visitors from abroad. For foreign visitors it may not just be a question of producing (say) a French or German version of a trial: some communities may have very specific links (often by way of immigration or emigration) with countries abroad. Illustrations are the Pilgrim Fathers; the successive waves of Protestant immigration from the Low Countries and France; trans-Atlantic emigration in the 19th and early 20th centuries during times of depression in the United Kingdom; and successive waves of Jewish immigration from Eastern Europe during the late 19th and early 20th centuries. If there are lingering traces of such trends they may well furnish suitable material for an interesting and unusual interpretive venture.

(3) MEDIA

The next stage is to consider how the range of interpretive media might be harnessed to the objectives which have been identified. Because of the financial implications the outcome of this analysis will be a key factor in determining the overall strategy.

The available media may be divided into those—like heritage centres and vantage point keys—which offer some kind of permanent display, and those—like trails and community biographies—which do not. The distinction is arbitrary because certain media in the second category (e.g. signed trails (9)) involve a display element. A profit, or at least a financial return, is possible on all media in this category, and also on heritage centres in the first category. The following list, though not exhaustive, will give some idea of the range of possibilities. The media (on which fuller advice is given subsequently) appear in inverse order of capital cost in each section, the most expensive coming first and the least costly last. The cost in each case is the *minimum* likely to be incurred, at *September 1978 prices.* More detailed information on both capital and running costs is given in Appendix 2, p 115.

Display Media

(1) HERITAGE CENTRE (£12,500+) A permanent exhibition occupying at least 2,000 sq ft and designed to give users (both residents and visitors) as full an insight as possible into the way in which a community has evolved to meet changing economic and social needs and to enable them to see for themselves how this evolution is reflected in the existing land-use pattern, street plan and fabric. To do its job properly a heritage centre needs to be backed up by such other media as trails or explorer's kits. It helps if it can be housed in a building which is of interest in itself. Running costs can be drastically cut if a centre is managed and manned by volunteers. The concept is a new one, introduced during European Architectural Heritage Year 1975, and there are at present nine centres—in Arundel, Ashford (Kent), Chester, Durham, Faversham, Ledbury, Pendle, Stockton, and York. In addition there are other recently-established facilities—such as the Ironbridge Visitor Centre, the Museum of Oxford and the two Landmark Centres in Scotland—which are similar in character and approach.

(2) DISPLAY CASES (WITH PERIODICALLY 'ROTATING' DISPLAYS) (£5,500 + for a set of four) Probably sited in a shopping centre or market place, these are weather- and vandal-proof showcases featuring a series of *changing* displays which highlight different aspects of an area's heritage in turn. The aim should be to enable anyone 'following' the series to learn nearly as much as they would from a heritage centre, and the themes might follow the same pattern and sequence. Three-dimensional material, such as models, samples of building materials, and bygones, can be featured as well as graphic displays.

(3) MINI HERITAGE CENTRE (£2,000 +) A permanent exhibition occupying at least 200 sq ft, designed to give users (both residents and visitors) a concise introduction to the way in which a community has evolved, and housed in part of a building (such as a town hall, railway station or church) already open to the public. Wherever it is housed, a mini heritage centre should take a starting point the building in which it is housed. Like a full-scale heritage centre, it needs to be backed up by such non-display media as trails or explorer's kits. It may be unstaffed, or part-time staffed, preferably by volunteers. A proprietary exhibition system may be used so that displays can be dismantled quickly when the space is needed temporarily for other purposes or when they are wanted for an occasional showing elsewhere in the area.

(4) AUDIO-VISUAL (£1,450 +) Audio-visuals are slide shows with a pre-recorded commentary which by means of a tape-slide synchroniser run automatically from beginning to end. They are a feature of most heritage centres but can also be provided independently elsewhere—e.g. in museums, town halls, information bureaux or any other suitable indoor locations to which the public have ready access and where staff may be prepared to operate them. An independent audio-visual may have the same aim as a mini-heritage centre—to introduce the viewer to the area—or it may focus attention on some narrower theme, such as the building in which it is housed.

(5) DISPLAY CASE (£1,375 +) A single display case with a permanent display may be sited in a big urban space such as a market place, square or quay to promote interest in the immediate area. Alternatively the case can be located in an indoor location such as a covered market or civic centre. The advantage of a case over a display board (7) is that three-dimensional material can be incorporated.

(6) VANTAGE POINT KEY (£300 +) These are already popular in the countryside. Good use of them can also be made in commanding positions with good views in towns and cities. Distant landmarks such as church towers, factory chimneys and even overhead power lines can reveal a good deal about the way a community has evolved.

(7) DISPLAY BOARD (£150 +) A single display board well sited serves a similar purpose to a display case (5).

Non-Display Media

(8) COMMUNITY BIOGRAPHY (£1,250 + for 1,000 copies) An attempt to outline the life-history of a community from the time of its first settlement to the present day, this is the published equivalent of a heritage centre (1). The aim should not be to compile an exhaustive account (which would involve years of research) but to identify the main strands in a community's development, describe them, and explain how they have been interwoven to influence the area's present fabric and life.

(9) LISTENING POSTS (£1,200 + for set of 4) A new medium developed by the Countryside Commission (England), the listening post is an electronic device enabling up to 4 people at a time to hear a pre-recorded commentary explaining what can be seen from a particular viewpoint. Built into the post, which is about a metre high, is a tape player and rechargeable battery. Users hire special acoustic 'listening tubes', plug these into one of the four outlets, and press a button to start the tape, which usually lasts about 2 minutes.

(10) SIGNED TRAIL (£700 + for 5,000 copies of the trail and the manufacture and installation of 16 plaques). This is a trail (15) where the leaflet is supplemented by informative wall plaques at key points. Alternatively or as well the trail may be signed by pavement markings, either stencilled on the footway or inlaid into it.

(11) HERITAGE GUIDE CARDS (£650 + for 1,000 copies each of 15 cards and 1,000 plastic wallets). Sets of cards are published on a theme or area and are available individually or in sets. Convenient in use, they also appeal to the collecting instinct.

(12) CONSERVATION AREA GUIDE (£625 + for 5,000 copies) A conservation area trail (15) which also explains how conservation areas are designated, why this particular one has been designated, and what this entails in the way of conservation and enhancement policies and measures.

(13) EXPLORER'S KIT (£600 + for 1,000 copies of 30 loose A4 sheets and 1,000 printed manilla wallets) Users are supplied with a basic route-plan supported by a sheet of notes and such documents (in reproduction) as photographs old and new, old prints, tradesmen's letterheads, timetables and press cuttings, which are keyed to the route plan. They use these to undertake their own detective work and draw their own conclusions.

(14) SOUND TRAIL (£595 + for 10 cassette players and all ancillary equipment) A trail (15) where the information instead of being printed is recorded on cassette and then available on hire (with a player) from a suitable central point. A disadvan-tage (unless printed notes are also available) is that the user retains no permanent memento, an advantage that if personal reminiscences and dramatised dialogue are introduced the trail has more immediacy.

(15) TRAIL (£300 + for 5,000 copies) Interesting features are highlighted along a pre-planned route.

(16) WALLSHEET (£250 + for 1,000 copies) A well-designed wallsheet is a good means of capturing the elements which give a community its distinctive character. Two popular forms are a bird's eye view and a mosaic or capriccio of buildings. In both cases informative but concise notes need to be superimposed on the artwork.

(17) GUIDED WALKS In the hands of a knowledgeable guide with a gift for imparting information in lively fashion a conducted tour can be one of the most effective media of interpretation. Among its advantages are that if guides are voluntary no outlay is needed and no payment is required from participants; that if the party is a coherent one in terms of age, interest or provenance, the scope and/or level of the treatment can be tailored to their needs; and, last but not least, that participants can seek, and usually obtain, immediate answers to questions the guide's commentary may stimulate.

It must be emphasised that this list is *not* exhaustive. Among other possible media for urban interpretation are mobile exhibitions (similar to mini heritage centres but designed to be on show successively in such locations as libraries, schools, community centres, banks and stores) and bus or train trails, where a guide is provided to what can be seen on an existing circular bus or train route or perhaps a couple of connecting routes which between them form a circuit.

It must also be stressed that the greatest care must be taken with the design and siting of any interpretive 'hardware'. A part from the fact that permission may be required from owners, and that planning permission or listed building consent may be needed from the local authority, there is a serious risk of the 'hardware' proving visually intrusive. It would be ironical, for example, if a display board which highlighted among other things the disruptive effect of superfluous traffic signs in a market place was so badly designed and/or sited that it only made matters worse.

The stage is now set for consideration of the media best suited to achieve the objectives identified. In some cases, to continue with Forchester as an illustration, more than one medium will suit a particular purpose. Thus 'Industry in Forchester' could serve as the theme of an audio-visual, a set of heritage cards, a trail, a sound trail or a wallsheet. All the various options should be listed against each possible topic.

(4) STRATEGY

The next stage is to draw up a realistic strategy for interpretation—in other words to decide what are the priorities, given the resources of cash and manpower likely to be available. Ideally in any community except the smallest the aim should be to draw up a five-year programme under which coordinated facilities can be provided. Research can then be coordinated, too, and it may be possible to 'stretch' available resources by devising some material (such as maps and drawings) in such a way that it can be used in more than one medium. Though resources may be slender it should be borne in mind that some media should yield a profit which can be ploughed back into the programme.

Issue-based objectives should enjoy top priority. Forchester, it seems clear, is a suitable setting for a heritage centre and the establishment of one towards the end of the five-year period should certainly be an aim, but in the immediate future there are particular problems towards the solution of which lower-cost interpretive initiatives can probably make an important contribution.

It helps to list these together with the media considered most suitable:

(a) Conservation area management
Mini heritage centres; audio-visuals; display boards; signed trails; sound trails; conservation area guides; wallsheets

(b) Derelict industrial sites and buildings
Mini heritage centre; audio visual; trail; wallsheet

(c) Central area churches and chapels
Mini heritage centre; audio visual; wallsheet

(d) Shopping centre
Display case; display boards; audio visual; wallsheet

The next step is to make a decision on media.

(a) Conservation Area Management
There are seven conservation areas in all. Because of the urgent need to widen appreciation the more elaborate and expensive media are discarded. In the end it is decided that a *conservation area guide* is most suitable for the Cliff area, where metal-framed windows are on the march, because helpful advice to householders can be neatly fitted in; *trails* for the two central areas (where the full potential for environmental improvement has yet to be realised and needs highlighting); and *wallsheets* for the four village centres, whose character is being eroded by the application of unidiomatic 'period' detail whose spuriousness can best be exposed by illustrating some of the buildings which have remained unviolated. An advantage is that the selected media will all earn revenue—with any luck result in a profit.

(b) Derelict industrial sites and buildings
Again the need for urgent action rules out costly media. The wallsheet is ruled out because it is unlikely to induce many people actually to look at the sites and buildings for themselves. The only answer is a *trail*. With any luck, too, this will yield a return, or at least meet its costs.

(c) Central area churches and chapels
Several of these buildings are in jeopardy and one main reason is that so few people have ever seen for themselves how attractive they are. Though some interest might be generated by an *audio-visual* (sited, say, in the town hall) it would be a mistake to miss the opportunity of housing special displays in each building. So with the co-operation of the clergy and congregations concerned it is decided that a *mini heritage centre* (confined to this special theme) should be provided in one church, and smaller *ancillary displays* in each of the others. If the necessary capital can be found, a *wallsheet* will also be published and placed on sale as a permanent memento. This should yield a profit which can be ploughed back for fabric maintenance. Given that the central area is now 'over-churched', the main display might suggest a range of suitable alternative uses for some of the buildings.

(d) Shopping centre
In this case an *audio-visual* seems the most effective way of bringing home the advantages of a traditional shopping centre such as the town still possesses. Some of the local craftsmen can be shown at work and their premises pinpointed. Contrasts with the bleak monumentality of some modern multi-level shopping centres elsewhere may stress the point that though indeed these have much to offer and reflect a prevailing scale of values they are not always preferable to traditional 'High Street' facilities. The possibilities of a *display case, display board* and *wallsheet* are considered, but discarded because they are less flexible than an audio-visual, where a 'dated' slide can be replaced in a matter of days and (if care is taken with the original drafting) no alteration in the recorded commentary may be necessary.

Though such issue-based objectives enjoy the highest priority it is also useful to make a short list of any of the others which might be tackled within the five-year period. After all if revenue-earning media can be adopted for some of these, the whole programme may be facilitated. In this light a series of *wallsheets* on such topics as Victorian Forchester, Forchester and the Railways, Forchester Yards and Courts, Forchester and the Industrial Revolution and Forchester Pubs and Clubs looks a particularly good prospect as initial outlay is low and elsewhere similar themes have proved to be very popular. Worth tackling but perhaps less likely to achieve steady sales are a couple of *trails* on the work of the town's two distinguished Victorian architects. Well produced and promoted, an *explorer's kit* might sell readily—and also serve as something of a 'dry run' for some of the themes to be included in a heritage centre. Finally though it would yield no financial dividend a *viewpoint key* overlooking the river at the Cliff would probably prove popular and might attract financial support from the Rotary Club, Round Table or Townswomen's Guild.

So far the programme's likely ingredients have been identified only by reference to *theme.* What about the audiences, the consumers? There is plenty of provision for those who live, work or shop in the town, but what about visitors, and children? In fact most of the ingredients will appeal almost as much to visitors as to local people, so since time and money are limited no special provision need be made. With children, however, it is a different matter. In a sense they know more matter adults, for in a few years' time they will be taking responsibility for the town's future function and shape, and the better-informed they are the better they will discharge this responsibility.

A quick scrutiny will show that *if* sufficient care is taken, many of the elements in the programme will interest the over-10s as much as their parents. Examples are the mini heritage centre, the wallsheets, the audio-visual, the explorer's kit and the viewpoint key. Provided these are not laced with too much abstruse learning or literary pyrotechnics (and they should not be, anyway) they will make their mark with the over-10s. Younger children probably need special provision and in collaboration with two or three sympathetic primary school teachers it is decided to try to produce a couple of discovery *kits*—basically trails designed to introduce the children to the core of the town, to get them to 'spot' some of its interesting features and salient characteristics.

In summary therefore these are thought to be the desirable elements in the first five-year programme (an asterisk * indicates that the selected medium might well yield a useful financial return):

Issue-based objectives
— *Conservation area guide* for the Cliff area
— *Trails* for each of the two central conservation areas
— *Wallsheets* for each of the four village conservation areas
— *Trail* to focus attention on the potential of derelict industrial buildings and sites
— *Mini heritage centre* in one of the central area churches and chapels, with *ancillary displays* in each of the others
— *Back-up *wallsheet*
— *Audio-visual* on the shopping centre and its facilities

Other objectives
— *Wallsheets* on Victorian Forchester, Forchester and the Railways, Forchester Yards and Courts, Forchester and the Industrial Revolution, and Forchester Pubs and Clubs
— *Trails* on the work of W Vernon Heysham and Matthew Morris
— *An *explorer's kit*
— A *viewpoint key* on the Cliff
— A pair of *discovery kits* to introduce primary school children to the core of the town

Long-term objective
— *Heritage Centre* (perhaps in one of the churches or chapels for which it looks as though a new use will have to be found?)

In which order should the programme be tackled and what scope does it offer for co-ordination of approach?

The order in which the schemes are undertaken depends partly on how urgently they are needed, partly on resources of cash and manpower. It has already been noted that priority should be given to issue-based schemes; money-raising is discussed below; and even if at least some skills have to be paid for there is usually little problem about finding suitable manpower for research, design, implementation and publicity.

Though (particularly for voluntary organisations) money-raising presents the biggest challenge, it is much easier to meet this challenge if, in the early stages of the programme, priority can be given to those elements which can earn revenue to be ploughed back into the later stages.

Fortunately in the case of Forchester (and there is no reason to believe it is unrepresentative) the need to begin with issue-based objectives is largely compatible with priority being given to revenue-earning media. In the end, after careful consideration of all the relevant factors, the programme looks like this.

— *Trail* to focus attention on the potential of derelict industrial buildings and sites. (It is recognised that this may only just cover its costs but the problem is probably the most urgent of all)

— *Conservation area guide* for the Cliff area
* Trails for each of the two central conservation areas
Wallsheets for each of the four village conservation areas
(As well as doing an important job, these should all sell very well, and with any luck will be reprinted several times to yield a steady return)

— The two *discovery kits* to introduce primary school children to the core of the town. (These are put in hand at an early stage to lay foundations of interest which can be developed by other media as the children grow older)

— *Wallsheets* on Victorian Forchester, Forchester and the Railways, Forchester Yards and Courts, Forchester and the Industrial Revolution, and Forchester Pubs and Clubs. (These should prove very popular and profitable—and this is why they are given priority over the other two issue-based objectives)

— *Mini heritage centre* in one of the central area churches and chapels, with *ancillary displays* in each of the others
*Back-up *wallsheet* (This will be an expensive venture and it will also take much longer to devise and create than any of its predecessors)

— *Trails* on the work of W Vernon Heysham and Matthew Morris. (These are more speculative than some earlier publications but may still yield a useful dividend).

— *Audio-visual* on the shopping centre and its facilities. (Of the issue-based schemes this is probably the least urgent, as the threat is more nebulous. As well as being expensive this will take a surprisingly long time to compile, as it will quickly emerge that to make their full impact certain shots can only be taken at certain times of the year)

— *Viewpoint key* on the Cliff

— *Explorer's kit* (The research for this will take a long time and it will be quite expensive to produce. Undertaken towards the end of the programme it can also feature useful cross-references to other initiatives already taken)

— *Heritage Centre* (This will be the biggest and most costly initiative of all. Even at the end of the five-year period its provision may have to be deferred. However much of the research for it will already have been done in connection with the other schemes and once the Centre is established it is an ideal sales point for all the interpretive material already in print)

Co-ordination of the elements in the programme is very important and of course it should look forward to future initiatives as well as back to ones that have already been undertaken. In terms simply of promotion for example the very first initiative—the trail featuring derelict industrial buildings and sites—should refer to the planned wallsheet on Forchester and the Industrial Revolution.

But there is more to it than cross-references of one kind and another. Though the elements take different forms it is important to establish from the first some 'house-style' of design and presentation that can be applied to all. Apart from helping to unify successive initiatives this will increase public interest, loyalty and confidence. Standards of design need to be high. Scrappily-designed material may actually alienate interest and (in the case of publications) is unlikely to sell well. At the same time it should be made clear that the framework is flexible and will not be slavishly followed if (for example) the need to highlight the advantages of the shopping centre becomes more urgent.

(5) MONEY-RAISING

A local authority or other public body which decides to undertake an urban interpretation programme is unlikely to organise a parallel money-raising campaign, though it may be eligible for grants from some of the sources described below. Provision will have to be made in the annual estimates in the usual way. Save in the case of a heritage centre the individual outlays are not large by local authority standards but, since proverbially in local government it is often the smallest allocations that generate the most heated controversy, it will help if each item can be seen in the wider context of a comprehensive interpretive programme to which the authority is committed. Fears about the value of such a programme can be alleviated, if need be, by reference to the authority's responsibilities for planning, the provision of amenities, the promotion of tourism and (in the case of a county council) education.

However, much interpretive work is likely to be undertaken by voluntary organisations and for them money-raising is a bigger challenge. How is it to be tackled? Basically there are two alternative methods and, except in the case of small schemes, both should probably be exploited. The first is simply for the society to raise money by social events, raffles (a voluntary organisation which regularly organises raffles must be registered with the district council under the Lotteries and Amusements Act 1976), sales, publications and so on.

These techniques are mostly well-tried and, though they often involve a lot of hard work, they can yield good dividends. If the object of the particular event or function is well publicised they can also help promote interest in it. A minor difficulty with most of these techniques is that they are also used by other voluntary organisations and therefore care has to be taken (for example) to avoid holding a fete on the very same day as a well-established one. Publications, on the other hand, constitute a territory where a local society is unlikely to experience much competition, where it can apply its knowledge of the area, where there is likely to be wide appeal, and where quite useful profits can be made. All of them—even picture postcards and Christmas Cards, with a local scene on the cover and a brief explanatory note inside—also serve as interpretive media. Detailed advice about fund-raising by these and similar means is given Appendix 3, p 124.

The other method of raising extra funds is to seek grants from other sources. It must be emphasised at the outset, however, that there is very little prospect of meeting the whole cost of a scheme by way of grants. The reason for this is simply that (quite rightly) all grant-making bodies expect those responsible for an initiative to find some of the funds required for it. This is not to say that in some cases grants may not meet 75% or even 80% of the cost but to achieve this level a voluntary organisation needs to be able to point to a good 'track record' with its other constructive ventures.

Grants for restoration and conversion purposes will be needed only in the event of a heritage centre being created in an historic building and advice about them is given later, in the appropriate chapter.

The range of possible sources of financial assistance for interpretive work is quite wide and the following a summary. Common sense dictates that the first approach to any organisation should be an exploratory one, giving clear but concise details of the project for which assistance is sought, and enquiring whether it is one to which consideration might be given. A preliminary approach of this kind saves everyone trouble if in the event it emerges that for whatever reason the particular organisation would be unable to consider a formal application.

Local Authorities
DISTRICT COUNCILS have powers to assist anyone providing *exhibitions* or *facilities for recreation* in their area (Local Government Act 1972 s 144; in Scotland, Local Government (Scotland) Act 1973, s 90); to assist anyone providing an *entertainment* of any nature (s 145; in Scotland, s 91); and to assist anyone providing facilities for the 'development and improvement of the knowledge, understanding and practice of the *arts and the crafts which serve the arts*' (s 145; in Scotland, s 91). They also have powers to contribute to any United Kingdom *charity* in furtherance of that charity's work (s 137; in Scotland, s 83); and (in England and Wales only, subject to an aggregate ceiling of the equivalent of a 2p rate) to 'incur expenditure which in their opinion is in the interests of their area or any part of it or all or some of its inhabitants' (s 137). However a grant from the 'free two pence' cannot be made for a purpose for which expenditure is explicitly authorised or required by other legislation.

In effect this means that a society wishing to obtain financial assistance for an interpretive project should get in touch with the District Council's Recreation and Entertainments Officer (or equivalent) to explore the possibility of grant-aid under one or other of these heads. Copies of any correspondence should be sent simultaneously to the Planning and Publicity (or Information) Officers, and personal discussions with local members and the Chairmen of appropriate Committees may well be helpful. If the project is part of a long-term programme this should be made clear, as it may enhance the chances of a grant and members or officers may have useful suggestions to offer. Though local authority spending is now (1979) severely restricted, an approach may still be worthwhile, if only because towards the end of council financial years there are sometimes sums available which have been earmarked for other purposes that have proved abortive. In any event it is possible to argue in some cases (e.g. that of a conservation area guide which gives advice as well as information) that an interpretive project may marginally reduce the workload imposed on council staff. At the same time, for obvious reasons, an authority is unlikely to offer a series of grants to a succession of ventures which are all likely to yield another organisation a substantial profit.

PARISH AND TOWN COUNCILS in England and Wales also enjoy these powers but of course their resources are much more limited. Occasionally, however, they may be able to make small contributions and approaches are most worthwhile to those few (mostly in towns) who make full use of their general powers.

COUNTY COUNCILS in England and Wales and REGIONAL COUNCILS in Scotland also enjoy these powers but some may expect the appropriate district councils to be primarily responsible for using them where a scheme mainly benefits a particular district. Others, however, particularly those with an active interest in conservation, might respond helpfully to proposals from a county federation of amenity societies for a series of interpretive initiatives on a county-wide basis. County and Regional Councils also have powers (s 141; in Scotland, s 87), which may be relevant, to assist anyone undertaking research into 'any matters concerning the county (in Scotland, their area) or any part of the county (in Scotland, their area)' and making available to the public the results of the research. As education and museum authority a county or regional council may also be able to offer grant-aid.

LOTTERIES It is possible, though perhaps not very likely, that a local authority which runs a lottery might be willing to make a small grant from the profits towards the cost of an interpretive venture, particularly a larger-scale one, if it was satisfied that it was in the interests of the local community to do it. (Under the Lotteries and Amusements Act 1976 a local authority may promote a local lottery 'for any purpose for which they have power to incur expenditure under any enactment.')

Tourist Boards

ENGLISH TOURIST BOARD can offer grants or loans, but *only* in the Special Development, Development, and Inter-mediate Areas (cf p 127) towards projects which will provide or improve tourist amenities or facilities. There are no hard-and-fast rules concerning the type of tourist attraction which can be considered and every application is dealt with on its merits. Projects aided so far range from light railways to information bureaux, from theatres to museum facilities. In addition a limited sum is available for 'Special Promotions' grants *anywhere* in England. In order to be eligible a scheme must be designed to enhance the visitor's enjoyment of his/her stay in the area, should ideally be innovative, should not involve building work, and should anticipate financial contributions from other sources as well as the Tourist Board. Applications should be made to the appropriate *Regional* Tourist Board:

Cumbria Tourist Board
 Ellerthwaite, Windermere, Cumbria
 (09662 4444)
East Anglia Tourist Board
 14 Museum Street, Ipswich IP1 1HU
 (0473 214211)
East Midlands Tourist Board
 Bailgate, Lincoln LN1 3AR
 (0522 31521)
Heart of England Tourist Board
 The Old Bank House, Bank Street, Worcester WR1 2EW
 (0905 29511)
London Tourist Board
 26 Grosvenor Gardens, London SW1W 0DU
 (01-730 3450)

Northumbria Tourist Board
 140/150 Pilgrim Street, Newcastle upon Tyne NE1 6TQ
 (0632 28795)
North West Tourist Board
 Last Drop Village, Bromley Cross, Bolton, Lancs BL7 9PZ
 (0204 591511)
South East Tourist Board
 4/6 Monson Road, Tunbridge Wells, Kent TN1 1NH
 (0892 40766)
Southern Tourist Board
 The Old Town Hall, Leigh Road, Eastleigh, Hants SO5 4DE
 (0703 616027)
Thames & Chiltern Tourist Board
 PO Box 10, Abingdon, Oxfordshire OX14 3HG
 (0235 22711)
West Country Tourist Board
 Trinity Court, Southernhay East, Exeter, Devon EX1 1QS
 (0392 76351)
Yorkshire & Humberside Tourist Board
 312 Tadcaster Road, York YO2 2HF
 (0904 707961)

SCOTTISH TOURIST BOARD offers grants and loans in the Special Development, Development, and Intermediate Areas (the whole of the country). Assistance is limited to 50% of the total cost of the project provided this does not bring the total subvention from public funds to more than 50% of the total. The Board's address is 23 Ravelston Terrace, Edinburgh EH4 3EU (031-332 2433).

WALES TOURIST BOARD offers grants and loans in the Development Areas (in effect, most of the Principality). However outside these areas it has no funds for 'Special Promotions'. The Board's address is Llandaff, Cardiff DY5 2YZ (0222 567701).

NORTHERN IRELAND TOURIST BOARD operates grants mostly through district councils, offering them at the rate of up to 75% towards the acquisition of land and up to 50% towards the cost of works. Grants of up to 33% of total cost may also be available direct from the Board, whose address is River House, 48 High Street, Belfast BT1 2DS (0232 31221).

HIGHLANDS AND ISLANDS DEVELOPMENT BOARD Within its area, which includes the Highland Region, part of Strathclyde Region (Argyll and Bute, and Arran) and the Orkney, Shetland and Western Islands areas, the *Highlands and Islands Development Board* offers financial assistance to projects of value to tourists. For recreational facilities of 'special development value' Special Grant in Tourism of up to 30% of eligible costs is available. Loans are also available at a favourable interest rate: the repayment period is up to 20 years in the case of buildings and up to 10 in other cases. Alternatively the Board may offer an Interest Relief Grant to reduced the cost of borrowing from commercial or other non-public sources. It can also offer advice on the development of recreational facilities. Any organisation considering the provision of such facilities would therefore be well advised to get in touch with the Board at the earliest opportunity. Enquiries should be addressed to the Tourism Division, Highlands and Islands Development Board, Bridge House, Bank Street, Inverness IV1 1QR (0463 34171).

Countryside Commissions

THE COUNTRYSIDE COMMISSION or the COUNTRYSIDE COMMISSION FOR SCOTLAND may be able to contribute towards interpretive work undertaken by local amenity societies and other voluntary organisations. To be eligible schemes must be for the interpretation of the countryside in England and Wales (most of the land area) or in Scotland in 'designated countryside' (which in practice covers 98% of the country excluding only parts of the larger towns and cities). Among schemes eligible for consideration would be those interpreting the countryside and the rural way of life at present or in the past in order to enhance understanding and appreciation of the countryside in general. In England the Countryside Commission has a specific policy of giving high priority to facilities designed to enable people to enjoy countryside on the urban fringes. Grant may be a fixed sum or a percentage of approved expenditure subject to a Commission's contribution not exceeding 75% of the total cost of the work.

In NORTHERN IRELAND no comparable grants are yet available.

The address of the Countryside Commission is John Dower House, Crescent Place, Cheltenham, Gloucestershire GL50 3RA; of the Countryside Commission for Scotland, Battleby, Redgorton, Perth PH1 3EW.

Charitable Trusts

CARNEGIE UNITED KINGDOM TRUST Under a three-year Heritage Interpretation Programme launched in March 1978 by the Carnegie United Kingdom Trust in association with the Civic Trust and Scottish Civic Trust, grants of up to 50% of the capital cost (and usually not exceeding £1,500) will be available to assist local amenity societies with interpretive projects. To be eligible, societies must be registered with the Civic Trust (17 Carlton House Terrace, London, SW1Y 5AW) or Scottish Civic Trust (24 George Square, Glasgow G2 1EF), from either of which further details are available. Applications

for grants towards the cost of heritage centres will be considered, but outside the main Programme.

OTHERS In England and Wales alone the estimated annual income of grant-making trusts (of which there are now more than 2,000) is £170,000,000. These figures, of course, are for trusts of all kinds, and many have specific objectives which preclude assistance to interpretive work. On the other hand the number is slowly increasing and it is worth bearing in mind that those with appropriate objectives may well be looking for good and imaginative schemes to help. The best guide to the interests and resources of trusts is the 'Directory of Grant-Making Trusts', published by the Charities Aid Foundation, 48 Pembury Road, Tonbridge, Kent TN9 2JD. Copies of this are available in most large reference libraries. It features as well as full details of each trust (in alphabetical order) lists classified by field of interest and geographical area. Thus the 'Directory' lists more than 200 trusts, large and small, empowered to make grants for general educational purposes, about 100 with power to assist the preservation of the countryside, and (perhaps significantly) just 27 with power to make grants for the preservation of amenities in cities, towns and villages. It has to be borne in mind, however, that the *precise* kinds of purpose for which trusts offer grants may vary when policies are adjusted by trustees. An organisation making application for grant under the Carnegie United Kingdom Trust/Civic Trust/Scottish Civic Trust Heritage Interpretation Programme may be able to obtain advice from the Trusts about other possible sources of grants for interpretive work.

Business and Industry

Approaches to larger local businesses and industries may often prove worthwhile. In the case of independently-owned firms (i.e. those which are not subsidiaries of national concerns) the first approach should probably be an informal one, to a member of the board. The same method may be adopted with subsidiary companies, though sometimes better results are yielded by an approach to the chairman of the parent or holding company. If a large retail chain has a sizeable store in the area, it is best to write direct to the chairman at head office. In some cases he or she may refer it to a family trust (almost certainly one of those listed in the 'Directory of Grant-making Trusts') and care should be taken to avoid approaching a firm when a request for assistance has already been made to the appropriate family trust.

Local amenity societies, whose active interest in the local environment may sometimes bring them into conflict with local firms, may be tempted to fight shy of seeking financial assistance from them on the ground that any grant might compromise their independence. Such a view is probably too narrow. In any application a society should of course make clear what are its basic aims and how it sets out to achieve them: otherwise in any case prospective donors will be unable to judge its character and standing. If the record is set straight in this way, it is doubtful whether any business concern could seriously suppose that any generosity on its part could confer immunity from criticism at a later date.

Other Sources

Particularly in the case of larger projects, it may be worth inviting such local organisations as Rotary, Round Table, and the Townswomen's Guild or Women's Institute to help with money-raising. In general the first two tend to be more favourably inclined to social welfare than environmental work (possibly because the latter is sometimes more controversial) but it should be borne in mind that environmental initiatives often carry with them social and economic benefits.

(6) RESEARCH

For every pint of interpretation, a gallon of research will often be needed. People who know a district well often think they know everything needed to compile a trail or conservation area guide. They realise how wrong they are as soon as they ask themselves what are the questions to which a visitor might require answers.

Take the example of the Cliff area in Forchester. As raw material this is actually less taxing than some other areas, for its was developed as a whole between about 1850 and 1885 and apart from the incursion of metal-framed windows has not changed outwardly since then. The challenge presented by the long and organic evolution of a town or village centre is much greater.

In all likelihood a quick raid on the standard histories of the town will yield little beyond the fact that the Cliff was built by the umpteenth Earl of Forchester on the site of a farm which had belonged to the family since the thirteenth century. With any luck there may be a mention of the architects involved; with a great deal more a builder or two may be named; and there may be a useful nugget of information such as that after completion of the local railway network many of the navvies found employment on the site. Hardly enough for a conservation area guide. The following are just a few of the questions which remain unanswered:

— People do not usually take wanton business risks. Why was the Cliff developed when it was?

— The general character of the area seems to have held up well. Is this because the houses were subject to ground-rent—or perhaps covenant?

— The landscaping as much as the architecture is responsible for the area's appeal. Whose is the credit?

— Though the street-plan is grand and basically symmetrical, there are some curious kinks. What constraints do these reflect?

— Though there is a riotous variety of house-types (no two are alike) the whole development possesses considerable unity and harmony. Why is this?

— Even at a time, like the present, when not many people can afford to live in big Victorian houses, the Cliff has not deteriorated as similar areas have elsewhere. Why is this?

— To this day there is not a single shop, pub or school in the area. Why is this and where do residents go for these facilities?

— Some of the earliest houses (and some of the most attractive) are in a homely 'domestic vernacular' style thirty years in advance of their time. They are unattributed. Who was the designer?

To most of these questions the answers will lie probably in old local directories and newspapers. In both, the advertisements are often nearly as informative as the editorial matter.

It emerges that with all the inherited acumen of the Forchesters the umpteenth Earl timed the first stages of the development to coincide with middle and upper management's burgeoning desire to quit their 18th century homes in the centre of the town for something in a more spacious and salubrious setting. The first few having established the fashion, others followed it for the next 35 years. Of the many such moves which can be traced in directories, one or two are quoted as illustrations in the finished guide. In fact the properties are freehold but subject to a particularly intimidating covenant whose provisions have held up mainly because of a Cliff Improvement Association thoughtfully founded by the umpteenth Earl and still in existence, though unbeknown to most people outside the area. For the name of the landscape architect the Forchester papers now in the county record office have to be searched. The name means nothing until reference to a work on the subject reveals that he was a pupil of J C Loudon and that not much is known about him. However the influence of the master is clear. Maps in the central reference library disclose that for each of the kinks in the street-plan there was a very good reason—Cliff Farm itself was not demolished until about 1880 for example (there even turns out to be a photograph of it) and there was a row of three windmills which also went on grinding flour long after half the fields had ceased growing wheat. One reason why the area is unified despite the range of house-types turns out to be that the umpteenth Earl was very fussy about the size (or 'mass') of the individual properties; another, more pertinent one, is that as vendor of each plot he stipulated that builders should use only stone from his own quarries and brick from his own brickfields. A shrewd businessman, and a good environmentalist into the bargain! It was he who saw to it too that there was not a shop, not a pub, not a school in the area. His motives here are less clear, but now as then residents are not inconvenienced for there is a long-established neighbourhood centre, with all three amenities, on the doorstep. The pub, needless to say, is the Forchester Arms. The architect of the unattributed houses turns out to be a long-forgotten colleague of the great Butterfield. In its way this is quite an important discovery and should rate at least a three-page feature in *Country Life* or the *Architectural Review*. And why has the area not deteriorated? A different kind of research is required to find the answer. It emerges that there *is* multi-occupation, and on quite a large scale, but mainly in the form of 'granny flats' in attics and basements. Far more are occupied by nurses and students than actual grannies but what has averted deterioration of the kind often associated with multi-occupancy is that the owners still occupy the remaining floors.

More demanding areas will pose a much wider range of questions, and it will not be nearly as easy to find answers in printed sources. Several visits, rather than a single one, may be required to the record office, but unless the researcher is a trained palaeographer great difficulty will be experienced with some pre-18th-century documents. All in all it may be best to comb methodically through what printed literature there is, in the hope perhaps that if the difficulties are actually acknowledge in the interpretive outcome it may encourage someone with the time and qualifications to extend this particular frontier of knowledge.

Research will also be required into the architectural character of the area's buildings. If they are listed, the descriptions in the Statutory Lists of buildings of special architectural or historic interest are the essential starting point. Copies of the List will be held by the district council's planning department and probably also in the local reference library. Local amenity societies often hold copies, too, but if they do not yet do so may be able to obtain them free of charge from the Department of the Environment, Scottish Office or Welsh Office as appropriate. (In Northern Ireland work on Statutory Lists began only in 1973 but for many districts the Ulster Architectural Heritage Society has produced its own admirable illustrated lists of buildings and areas of architectural importance. These are available by purchase from the Society at 181a Stranmillis Road, Belfast, BT9 5DU).

Particularly for pre-Victorian buildings the volumes (where published) of the Royal Commissions on Ancient and Historical Monuments of England, Scotland and Wales are an invaluable source of detailed information.

As well as describing the buildings the conservation area guide will need to relate them to the contemporary architectural climate and to offer some analysis of their aesthetic appeal. One or both of these jobs may already have been done in brief if there is a 'Pevsner' (Penguin Buildings of England series) which covers the district. However for the present purpose a more detailed treatment will be necessary. The buildings will have to be looked at to see what elements contribute to their quality (good proportion? ingenious use of materials? skilful massing? picturesque skylines? and so on). An effort will also need to be made to relate them to design trends prevailing at the time. In general are they typical of one or other of the successive Victorian revival styles; in particular do they seem influenced by, and/or to have been an influence upon, a similiar development elsewhere? Were some of the individual designs filched, with or without minor modifications, from one of the architectural pattern books of the period?

Almost any research of this kind will soon reveal gaps in background knowledge. When (and why) was the brick tax imposed, and lifted? What exactly was Coade Stone? What was a union and how did the term come to be applied to a workhouse? What was involved in the turnpiking of a road? What was a National School? What was a Court of Pie Powder and how did it get this name?

The following are among books which may be useful when such questions have to be answered (those marked with an asterisk * are out of print but may be borrowed from libraries):

General

M D Anderson, **History by the Highway,** Faber, 1967
Automobile Association, **Book of the British Countryside,** 1976
T C Barker and C I Savage, **An Economic History of Transport in Britain** (two volumes), Hutchinson, 3rd edition, 1975
Bland, Bell and Tawney, **English Economic History – Select Documents,** Bell, 1914 (paperback)
R A Buchanan, **Industrial Archaeology in Britain,** Penguin, 1972 (paperback); Allen Lane, 1974 (hardback)
G B G Bull, **A Town Study Companion,** Hulton, 1969
H Carter, **The Study of Urban Geography,** Edward Arnold, 2nd edition, 1976 (paperbacks)
*Francis Celoria, **Teach Yourself Local History,** English Universities Press, 1958

C W Chalklin, **The Provincial Towns of Georgian England: A Study of the Building 1740-1820,** Arnold, 1974

*Sir John Clapham, **Concise Economic History of Britain to 1750,** Cambridge University Press, 1957

Dorothy Davis, **A History of Shopping,** Routledge, 1966

H J Dyos (ed), **The Study of Urban Geography,** Arnold, 1976 (paperback)

H J Dyos and Michael Wolff, **The Victorian City** (two volumes), Routledge, 1977 (paperback)

Alan Everitt (ed), **Perspectives in English Urban History,** Macmillan, 1973

Margaret Gelling, **Signposts to the Past: Place-Names and the History of England,** Dent, 1978

John Haddon, **Discovering Towns,** Shire Publications, 1970 (paperback)

John Haddon, **Local Geography in Towns,** Philip, 1971

J B Harley, **The Historian's Guide to Ordnance Survey Maps,** Bedford Square Press, 1980

Haydn's Dictionary of Dates and Universal Information, Dover Publishing, 1969

W G Hoskins, **Local History in England,** Longman, 2nd edition, 1973 (paperback)

W G Hoskins, **English Landscapes,** BBC, 1973

W G Hoskins, **The Making of the English Landscape,** Penguin, 1973

Kenneth Hudson, **Industrial Archaeology,** John Baker, 1963

David Iredale, **Discovering Your Family Tree,** Shire Publications, 1975 (paperback)

*Geoffrey Martin, **The Town,** Studio Vista, 1961

Peter Mathias, **The First Industrial Nation: An Economic History of Britain 1700-1914,** Methuen, 1969 (paperback)

J B Mitchell, **Historical Geography,** English Universities Press, 1954

Ray Pahl, **Patterns of Urban Life,** Longman, 1970

*M M Penstone, **Town Study,** National Society's Depository, 1910

Arthur Raistrick, **Industrial Archaeology: An Historical Survey,** Eyre Methuen, 1972

John Richardson, **The Local Historian's Encyclopaedia,** Historical Publications Ltd., 1974 (paperback)

Alan Rogers, **Approaches to Local History,** Longman, 2nd edition, 1977 (paperback)

Alan Rogers (ed), **Group Projects in Local History,** Dawson, 1977

L F Salzman, **English Industries of the Middle Ages,** Pordes, 1964 (facsimile reprint)

L F Salzman, **English Trade in the Middle Ages,** Pordes, 1964 (facsimile reprint)

*Thomas Sharp, **The Anatomy of the Village,** Penguin

Arthur E Smailes, **The Geography of Towns,** Hutchinson, 1964

L Dudley Stamp, **Britain's Structure and Scenery,** Collins, 1946

D Stenhouse, **Understanding Towns,** Wayland, 1977

Sidney and Beatrice Webb, **English Local Government** (eleven volumes), Cass, 1963 (facsimile reprints)

Eric S Wood, **Collins Field Guide to Archaeology in Britain,** Collins 1963

Architecture, Building and Planning

W Ashworth, **The Genesis of Modern British Town Planning,** Routledge 1968 (third impression)

Michael Aston and James Bond, **The Landscape of Towns,** Dent 1976

*Colin and Rose Bell, **City Fathers: The Early History of Town Planning in Britain,** Penguin, 1972 (paperback)

M W Barley, **The English Farmhouse and Cottage,** Routledge, 1967 (2nd impression)

Maurice Beresford, **New Towns of the Middle Ages,** Lutterworth Press, 1967

Hugh Braun, **Parish Churches,** Faber, 2nd edition, 1974 (paperback)

Hugh Braun, **Old English Houses,** Faber, 1969 (paperback)

R W Brunskill, **Illustrated Handbook of Vernacular Architecture,** Faber, 1978 (2nd edition) (paperback and hardback)

R W Brunskill and Alex Clifton-Taylor, **English Brickwork,** Ward Lock, 1977

Gerald Burke, **Townscapes,** Pelican, 1976 (paperback)

Gordon E Cherry, **The Evolution of British Town Planning,** Leonard Hill, 1974.

Alec Clifton Taylor, **The Pattern of English Building,** Faber, 1972 (hardback and paperback)

H M Colvin, **Biographical Dictionary of English Architects 1660-1840,** John Murray, 2nd edition, 1978

*Gordon Cullen, **Townscape,** Architectural Press, 1964

D B Cullingworth, **Town and Country Planning in Britain,** Allen & Unwin, 1976

James Stevens Curl, **English Architecture: An Illustrated Glossary,** David and Charles, 1977

Gillian Darley, **Villages of Vision,** Architectural Press, 1977

J G Dunbar, **Historic Architecture of Scotland,** Batsford, 1978

Peter Eden, **Small Houses in England 1520-1820,** Historical Association 1969 (paperback)

Fleming, Honour and Pevsner, **Penguin Dictionary of Architecture,** Penguin, 2nd edition, 1972

Sir Banister Fletcher, **A History of Architecture,** revised by J C Palmes, 18th edition, 1975

John Gloag, **The Architectural Interpretation of History,** Black, 1975

Richard Harris, **Discovering Timber-Framed Buildings,** Shire Publications, 1978 (paperback)

*John Harvey, **English Medieval Architects: A Biographical Dictionary to 1550,** Batsford, 1954

John Harvey, **The Perpendicular Style,** Batsford, 1978

E P Hennock, **Fit and Proper Persons: Ideal and Reality in 19th Century Urban Government,** Arnold, 1973

John B Hilling, **The Historic Architecture of Wales,** University of Wales Press, 1976

David Iredale, **Discovering Your Old House,** Shire Publications, 1977 (paperback)

Ewart Johns, **British Townscapes,** Edward Arnold, 1965

Osbert Lancaster, **Pillar to Post: English Architecture without Tears,** John Murray, 1956

Nathaniel Lloyd, **A History of the English House,** Architectural Press, 1975 (facsimile reprint)

R T Mason, **Framed Buildings of England,** Coach Publishing House, 1975 (paperback)

Colin McWilliam, **Scottish Townscape,** Collins, 1975

Lewis Mumford, **The City in History,** Pelican, 1966 (paperback)

Vanessa Parker, **The English House in the 19th Century,** Historical Association, 1970 (paperback)

John & Jane Penoyre, **Houses in the Landscape,** Faber & Faber, 1978

Glen L Pride, **Glossary of Scottish Building,** Scottish Civic Trust, 1976

John Prizeman, **Your House: The Outside View,** Blue Circle Group 1975, (Portland House, Stag Place, London, SW1)

*J T Smith and E M Yates, **On the Dating of English Houses from External Evidence,** Field Studies (E W Classey Ltd), 1974

Sir John Summerson, **Georgian London,** Peregrine, 1978 (paperback)

Neville Whittaker, **House and Cottage Handbook,** Civic Trust for the North East, 1976

Jane A Wight, **Brick Building in England to 1550,** John Baker, 1972

Doreen Yarwood, **The Architecture of Britain,** Batsford, 1976

Among series of books which may be helpful are:

Batsford Guides to Industrial Archaeology (by region)

*Cambridge University Press **County Geographies** (published mostly between 1910 and 1930 but still useful)

David & Charles: **Industrial Archaeology of the British Isles** series (by area)

Greater London Council: **Survey of London** (by historic parish)

*Homeland Association **Homeland Handbooks** (published mostly between 1900 and 1939 and by far the best series of town guides ever published)

Longman: **Industrial Archaeology** series (by theme)

***Murray's Guides** (by county: published mostly between 1850 and 1900 but still invaluable)

Pelican History of Art (architecture volumes)

Shell Guides (by county)

Victoria County History (by area, then by theme)

***Weale's Practical Treatises** (by theme; published mainly between 1850 and 1900 but still useful for information on traditional building techniques)

It is worth bearing in mind that schools might be able to help with research. Thanks to the efforts of the Town and Country Planning Association, the Heritage Education Group (serviced by the Civic Trust) and others, environmental education is now being given higher priority in many schools. With the encouragement of sympathetic staff, older children may be able to undertake useful fieldwork and research. Some schools, indeed, have already been responsible for useful interpretive work—for example, producing trails of a high standard.

(7) IMPLEMENTATION

With research and money-raising complete, work can start on the creation of the interpretive material. A combination of writers, designers, artists, photographers, craftsmen, builders and printers will be involved, depending on the medium. For any project a brief is essential, if only as a discipline, to clarify thoughts. This applies even when (as in the case of a voluntary organisation) the material is being created as an 'in-house' job.

The brief should give concise but clear instructions about the purpose of the project, the medium selected, the funds available and the timescale, and supply background information about the client, with the name of its responsible representative. Those responsible for the creation of the material must be left a free hand to use their skills in the way that seems to them best calculated to achieve the desired objective (bearing in mind constraints of money and time) and once the job has been handed over to them there must be no interference. At the same time the client must be prepared to give whatever help may be required. In practice a designer or writer who is in doubt about a particular point usually has the sense to consult the client about it, so there is little risk of the finished product ending up as a travesty of what the client intended.

It may help to give an example of what is required. When it came to commission its guide for the Cliff conservation area the Forchester Society found that within its own membership it had a competent graphic designer, writer, photographer and artist, and that all were generously willing to give their services free of charge for the venture. It still provided them with a brief because this seemed the most businesslike way of tackling the scheme. This brief is printed overleaf (pp 50-53).

If a 'house-style' has already been formulated for the interpretive programme the designer will also have to be advised to work within it. If not he may be asked to use this opportunity to devise one, and his attention will need to be drawn to the other elements in the programme to which it is to be applied. Though the whole point of involving someone with design skills is to take advantage of them, the client may have certain guidance to offer. For example it might stipulate—and wisely—that techniques creating a feeling of nostalgia should be avoided (for example, a cover or title page whose phraseology is a long-winded pastiche of 18th-century work). For the majority, such devices will serve only as a barrier, and suggest that the area concerned has somehow been embalmed.

Design is all important, but so complex a subject that it cannot be discussed here in detail. Invariably the best results will be achieved by involving a designer with a good 'track record' in communications. In the case of publications a printer may sometimes have someone on the staff who can offer help. Elementary rules are to use one basic typeface throughout; not to cram pages up to the margins; to ensure that the type is big enough to read; to number pages; and to ensure that

(continued on page 54)

THE FORCHESTER SOCIETY

registered with the Civic Trust

Client
: The Forchester Society is a local amenity society registered with the Civic Trust. Its main objects are to stimulate public interest in the town and surrounding area; to promote high standards of architecture and planning within it; to preserve features worthy of retention; and to improve those which are indifferent. A voluntary organisation, it was formed in 1967 and has 440 members (96 of them living in the Cliff area). In 1969 it was instrumental in averting the demolition of Warrender House, a fine Victorian building in the High Street (now used as an annexe to the Council offices), and between 1974 and 1977 with help from other local organisations it re-opened to navigation the Forchester arm of the Grand Midland Canal.

Purpose
: The Forchester Society is keen to see the Cliff conservation area conserved and enhanced for the benefit of present and future generations. In the long term it believes this objective is most likely to be achieved by promoting the widest possible understanding of the qualities of urban and landscape design which give the area its distinctive character.

The area was developed for residential purposes on a spacious plan between 1850 and 1885 and is characterised by its skilful landscaping (now mature) and large Victorian houses in a wide range of styles which still contrive to harmonise with one another. Though not of national significance, the Cliff ranks high in the region among developments of its kind.

A particular trend now threatening to undermine the character of individual buildings (and ultimately of the area) is the substitution of metal-frame windows for the original wooden sashes and casements. The Society wishes to advise householders that besides being detrimental to the appearance of their properties such changes may also reduce their market value. This message applies to many other areas in the rest of the town - and beyond.

Though the term 'conservation area' has been in use for some years (and the Cliff was designated as such in 1972) its precise significance and implications are not always understood and the Society wishes to outline these.

Medium

The Society has decided after considering alternatives that a conservation area guide is the best medium for achieving these particular objectives. The guide is to incorporate a circular trail, highlighting features of interest. This should refer not only to architecture but also to the physical setting and social and economic factors; past and present.

Its financial calculations have been based on the assumption that the guide will take the form of an A5 16-page booklet printed offset-litho in one colour on coated paper with a card cover and having about 12 illustrations, one of them a street plan, and that 5,000 copies will be printed. It was calculated that these might cost about £625 exclusive of design, artwork, photography and editorial work.

In accordance with the Society's objective, one copy of the guide will be distributed by it free of charge to all owners and occupiers of property in the Cliff. It is estimated that 900 will be needed for this purpose, and a further 300 will be retained for distribution to those who acquire an interest in the area over the next four years. The remaining stock will be sold by the Society and through retail outlets in the town, it is expected at about 25p each.

The Society was much impressed by the style and content of the conservation area guide produced a year ago by the Winkford Civic Trust and a copy of this is attached. Though of course the designer is free to adopt a different format and style of presentation, the Society considers this a useful model. It also expects him to bear in mind that what is required is not an elaborate booklet with a high unit cost, but a workmanlike one whose cover price is sufficiently modest not to restrict sales to the better-off.

Funds

By its own efforts and from grants the Society has raised the sum of £625. No more than this is to be spent. An important point is that the Society is keen to see the guide produced as a 100% local product. Therefore it does not wish estimates to be obtained from printers outside the town.

Source Material

For the past six months while money-raising has been going on a small study-group led by the Vice-Chairman has been accumulating source material on the Cliff and its social, economic and cultural context. This includes photocopies of maps of the area before, during and after its development; photographs of the area old and new; written information about the area's history (up to the present day); relevant extracts from its sound archive of reminiscences of the town; and analyses of the design and lay-out of individual buildings. This material has been neatly arranged and classified and will be freely available. While some of the photographs have been taken purely for record purposes, others have been taken with an eye to pictorial quality and it is intended that in order to conserve funds a selection of these should be used in the guide. If an extract from an Ordnance Survey map is used permission and a fee will of course be required (application should be made to the Copyright Section, Ordnance Survey, Romsey Road, Maybush, Southampton SO9 4DH (0703 775555 extension 338)).

Timescale

Given that it is now early November, the Society considers it reasonable to expect delivery of the guide by Easter. April 10 marks the 130th anniversary of the formal commencement of the Cliff development and the Society plans to commemorate this by launching the guide.

Special Notes

In the course of research for the guide the Society has established that many of the original sash and casement windows in houses in the Cliff conform to a small range of standard patterns and sizes. Aware that one of the main reasons why householders instal metal-frame windows is that they can often be bought 'off the peg' (while authentic replacements have to be custom built at much greater expense) the Society has arranged with a sympathetic local joinery manufacturer for authentic replacements of the most common types to be available to order and at reduced cost. Details of this arrangement are to be released to the Press when the guide is launched on 10 April, and should be included in the text.

The Conservation Officer, Area Development Control Officer and Area Technical Services Officer of the Borough Council have offered help and advice with those sections of the guide which reflect their

respective interests, and consultation with them should therefore
take place at an early stage.

The Conservation Officer has indicated that the Borough Planning
Committee will give sympathetic consideration to applications for
grant under the Historic Buildings (Local Authorities) Act 1962
towards the cost of idiomatic restoration of properties in the area;
and also that through him the Committee will be pleased to endorse
any application for Conservation Grant for similar purposes sub-
mitted by householders to the Historic Buildings Council. A note
to this effect should be given prominence in the guide.

<u>Main</u>   The Vice-Chairman of the Forchester Society
<u>Contact</u>   (W V Hughes, Esq)
                       24 Church Row
                       Burton Russell
                       Forchester
                       (home telephone no. Forchester 54956)
                       (work telephone no. Thornhead 253)

(continued from page 49)

correlations between text and illustrations are clearly indicated. If both half-tone and line illustrations are used juxtapositions need to be very carefully handled, or there is a risk that an illustration of one kind may 'kill' one of the other alongside or above it.

It is worth bearing in mind, if professional design advice is needed but not available within the sponsoring organisation, that it may often be obtained by way of a 'live project' from a college of art. Graphic design students used to being given notional assignments for hypothetical clients will often welcome the opportunity of being offered a real brief as a result of which their work will actually be put to use. Alternatively, in the case of the more modest schemes it may be possible to enlist the co-operation of a local secondary school. Apart from its intrinsic value, any design work undertaken by the students may help them understand their own environment better.

Artists involved in interpretive work will normally be required to use their talents to give clear rather than impressionistic images of the subjects. Wispy watercolours or racy sketches rarely have a role in interpretation. The value of the artist is that his work can highlight some particular quality or architectural motif far better than any photograph; or create, on the basis of existing illustrative and documentary material, a vivid reconstruction of some view which disappeared decades ago.

Photographers, too, must remember that for interpretive purposes they are illustrators, seeking to capture the significant qualities of a particular subject. This is by no means as easy as it sounds, and in one important respect the photographer's job is more difficult than the artist's—for except within very narrow limits he cannot manipulate his image. To bring out the qualities of a building which depends for its effect largely on light and shade he may have to use his camera during a comparatively short period in the year (and of the day) when this effect is most apparent. The first time he tries to take the picture he may find that scaffolding has gone up overnight; the second time he may find its place taken by a row of parked cars. In these circumstances many an amateur photographer would still take the shot, only noticing when the proof print emerged that the cars rather than the building appeared to be the main subject. Even quite small 'incidents' such as no-parking signs or builder's boards, though unnoticed when the shot is taken, effectively 'kill' it for reproduction purposes, simply because they are distractions. Nor is it always as easy as it seems at first sight to take a general view capturing the essence of a particular street of vista. The light turns out to be flat, or so disproportionately strong on one side that the other is under-exposed and lacking in detail. Sometimes the sky or too prominent a shadow across the road surface dominates the picture. Even if lighting conditions are good, the shot may lack depth. This can be avoided by 'framing' it with a foreground feature such as foliage or a structural feature. A low camera level will reduce carriageway dominance while sometimes an upper-floor vantage point is the best means of capturing the shape of a street. Further advice on environmental photography is given in Appendix 4 (p 128).

The text must be taut and crystal-clear, whatever the medium. In most cases writers will be working within tight limits of space and if research has been done well the job of distillation will seem daunting–how do you cram not a quart but a gallon into a pint pot? The answer may well be that even after careful planning the first draft is double the required length, but this is no great disadvantage as it does ensure that the final text contains the essence of what needs to be said, and probably also that expression is lucid and free of extravagance.

It is important to remember that implementation of such schemes as signed trails, display boards and vantage point keys will be impossible without the consent of property owners and the local planning authority. These should be sought while research and fund-raising are still going on and in many cases it will be wise to begin with an informal approach. When the time comes for a formal request plans will be required and these need to be explicit and well-presented. If they are not, delays are inevitable.

(8) PUBLICITY

The launch of any interpretive project needs to be accompanied by well-planned publicity. However this is not the end of the matter. Publicity must be sustained for as long as the project is in operation.

Basically there are three possible elements:

- **(a) Publicity for the launch**
- **(b) Paid advertising thereafter**
- **(c) Promotion (free publicity) thereafter.**

(a) Publicity for the launch

A press notice issued four or five days in advance (or a week or two in the case of a larger schemes) is essential for every interpretive project. In some cases it may be preceded by a 'trailer' press notice issued a month or two beforehand. In many cases there may be a strong argument for a press notice at the beginning of the research stage. Apart from the fact that there will be a genuine need for background information this can also provoke general interest in the project as a whole.

For more ambitious schemes it is a good idea to arrange a press conference. This need not be on a grand scale (in the event maybe only a handful of reporters and photographers may attend) but it will give the Press an opportunity of meeting those involved. It is still true that 'human interest' gives a story a vividness it would otherwise lack.

In certain cases a 'state visit' may be arranged as well as a press conference. For example if any kind of trail is being published it makes excellent sense to invite a party of leading local figures to inaugurate it.

However modest the scheme the greatest care need to be taken over the drafting of press notices and the organisation of press conferences or 'state visits'. There is nothing worse than a press notice which waxes eloquent about an initiative but fails to say who was responsible for it, or about a press conference or 'state visit' which is ill-organised or timed to coincide with an established local event traditionally attended by the full complement of local dignitaries. If the project is part of a long-term programme, this should be clearly stated in the press notice and reiterated at any press conference.

It is always best to draft a press notice in such a way that if necessary the body of it can be used *verbatim*. Reporters are busy people and on a local weekly or evening paper a press notice stands a good chance of being printed *verbatim* if it is tidy, lively and contains all the necessary information. However, to make any necessary editing easier it should be typed in 1½ spacing, on one side of the paper only, and with plenty of white space in the margins.

Advice on local distribution is probably unnecessary—most organisations already have a well-established list—but if wider circulation is required it is useful to refer to Benn's Press Directory, Volume 1, which lists local radio and TV stations as well as almost all newspapers and periodicals published in the U.K. It is often helpful to tip off individual reporters ahead of the formal press notice.

An example of a press notice, (issued by the Forchester Society to mark the publication of the Cliff Conservation Area Guide), is printed overleaf (pp 56–58).

(b) Paid advertising after the launch
(c) Promotion (free publicity) after the launch

The range of possibilities is perhaps best indicated in a table. Priorities are indicated by the figures 1 (essential), 2 (desirable) and 3 (useful). Where no figure is given, a particular technique is low-priority or inapplicable.

	Press notice	Press conference	Posters	Handbill	Car-sticker	Newspapers	Magazines	Annuals	TV/Radio	Other interpretive media	Street plan	Town guide	Tourist leaflet	Guidebooks/annuals	Special visits	Special displays	Souvenirs
Display media																	
1 Heritage centre	1	1	3	1	3	3	2	2	3	1	1	1	1	1	1	1	1
2 Display cases (set)	1	3	–	–	–	–	–	–	–	1	–	1	2	1	2	3	2
3 Mini heritage centre	1	2	3	1	–	3	3	3	–	1	1	1	1	1	2	3	2
4 Audio visual	1	2	3	2	–	–	–	–	–	1	–	1	1	2	2	–	3
5 Display case	1	–	–	–	–	–	–	–	–	1	–	1	3	3	3	3	2
6 Vantage point key	1	–	–	–	–	–	–	–	–	1	2	1	2	–	1	–	3
7 Display board	1	–	–	–	–	–	–	–	–	1	–	2	2	3	2	–	3
Other media																	
8 Community biography	1	2	–	–	–	3	3	–	–	1	–	3	3	3	3	2	3
9 Listening post	1	2	1	1	–	–	–	–	–	1	2	1	1	1	1	2	2
10 Signed trail	1	1	–	3	2	–	3	3	–	1	–	1	2	2	1	2	2
11 Heritage guide cards	1	2	3	2	–	3	3	–	–	1	–	1	2	2	2	2	2
12 Conservation area guide	1	2	–	3	3	3	3	–	–	1	–	1	2	2	1	2	2
13 Explorer's kit	1	2	–	3	–	3	3	–	–	1	–	1	2	2	1	2	2
14 Sound trail	1	2	1	1	2	3	3	3	–	1	–	1	1	1	1	2	2
15 Trail	1	2	–	–	3	–	3	3	–	1	–	1	1	2	1	2	2
16 Wallsheet	1	–	–	–	–	3	3	–	–	1	–	1	2	2	–	3	–
17 Guided walks	1	3	3	2	–	–	–	–	–	1	–	1	2	2	1	2	2

(continued on page 59)

THE FORCHESTER SOCIETY

registered with the Civic Trust

P R E S S   N O T I C E

embargoed till 0800 hrs, Thursday 10 April

NEW GUIDE HIGHLIGHTS TOWN'S VICTORIAN HERITAGE

Published today (Thursday) by the Forchester Society is a new illustrated booklet (copy attached) highlighting the fascinating Cliff area of the town, developed in Victorian times.

THE CLIFF CONSERVATION AREA GUIDE is the fruit of hundreds of hours' work by Society members - researchers, writers and illustrators - who all gave their time free of charge. It aims to pinpoint the qualities which give the area its distinctive character in the hope that if these are more widely understood and enjoyed there will be less chance of their being eroded.

This is the second initiative taken by the Society in its new five-year FORCHESTER HERITAGE programme. The first, published six months ago and still available price 10p, was the eye-opening CHALLENGE TRAIL, which prompted the Borough Council to form a special group to tackle the problem of derelict industrial sites close to the town centre. Next in the series will be trails and wallsheets for conserv-ation areas and in the longterm the Society hopes to provide a full-scale Heritage Centre for the town.

'Though the Cliff has been a popular residential area for well over 100 years,' says the introduction to the guide published today, 'there are many people in the town who hardly know it and probably do not realise that in this part of the country it is one of the most attractive areas of its kind.'

How was the area developed? Who was responsible? What was on the site before? Who moved into the properties when they were first built? What does conservation area status mean? These are just a few of the questions answered in the new booklet, which is the first ever published on the Cliff.

Co-ordinating work on the guide was Society Vice-Chairman Bill Hughes. 'We hope people have as much fun using it as we had putting it together', he said. 'We made some interesting discoveries - for example that some of the area was still being farmed in the 1880s and that there were once three windmills on the rise at the top of Belvedere Road. Points like this are mentioned in the trail we have included in the guide. This is a circular walk, taking about 45 minutes which we think will be very popular.'

A particularly attractive feature of the booklet are the drawings by Society member Sue Wilkins. 'As well as trying to capture the spirit of the whole I've drawn attention to some of the charming features that can easily be missed - like the handsome front doors most of the properties still have. People can't afford craftsmanship of this kind today. One thing is a bit of a pity, though. Some of the original windows have been replaced by metal-frames looking as silly as a feather hat on a weather-beaten farmer'.

People put the metal-frame windows in because they can be bought 'off the peg'. However, the guide contains good news for Cliff householders. The Society has arranged with a local joinery manufacturer for authentic window replacements to be available at reduced cost, and details are given of how these can be obtained.

Important news, too, is contained in the explanation of conservation area status. The Borough Council may be able to offer grants towards the cost of sympathetic restoration, and its Conservation Officer can offer advice about technical problems.

Cost of the new guide (printed by the Forringham Press) was met by the Society. It will be distributed free of charge by members to all owners and occupiers of property in the Cliff, and copies are also on sale in local bookshops and newsagents, price 25p.

NOTES FOR EDITORS

1. To mark the launching of the guide two special events have been arranged. On Saturday 12 April at 11 a.m. a party consisting of the Mayor, members and leading officers of the Borough Council, the MP, and officials of leading local organisations will formally inaugurate the Cliff trail. For four weeks from Saturday there will also be special display on the Cliff in the Central Library entrance lobby.

2. Later in the year the Society hopes to arrange an 'Open House Day' when half a dozen members who live in the Cliff will open their properties to the public. A descriptive brochure, available beforehand at about 25p, will admit to all properties.

3. Background information about the Society is enclosed for your information.

FOR FURTHER INFORMATION

Bill Hughes (Vice-Chairman) Forchester 54956 (work Thornhead 253)
Sue Wilkins - Forchester 52287

(continued from page 55)

It is worth saying a word about each of these techniques.

(b) Paid advertising

Posters are quite expensive to produce and, unless funds are available for display on commercial hoardings and drums, can be difficult to place permanently. They are probably essential only for sound trails, where prominent advertising will be needed in hotels, libraries, bus and railway stations and at the hire-point.

Handbills are essential to attract visitors to the larger-scale indoor displays and also to back up poster advertising of sound trails. They are quite cheap to print and because of their small size (A5 is ideal) are easy to place permanently on non-commercial sites. It is a good idea to insert them with routine correspondence—provided of course some discrimination is used and copies are not sent repeatedly to the same addressee.

Car-stickers are never essential but can be useful as they travel far and wide and are often on show for long periods when a vehicle is parked in a prominent place. They are cheap to print. Sometimes the cost can be recovered, and a small profit made, by selling them as souvenirs.

Newspaper advertising can certainly help to create a market if the product is good enough and of sufficient general interest. However since repeated insertions of an advertisement at least 5cm deep in double column are needed, it is costly.

Magazine advertising is a slightly better proposition, partly because magazines tend to have a longer life than newspapers, partly because many come out monthly rather than weekly and costs are lower. There is little point in taking space in any general-interest magazine but advertising in one devoted to a particular county or relevant special subject can yield useful dividends. Series reductions make repeated insertions cheaper. Since magazines are printed on better-quality paper the opportunity should be taken of including an illustration, if possible.

Annuals such as tourist board guides and museum directories are a good place to advertise larger-scale indoor displays and sound trails. Illustrations are essential if the best advantage of the space is to be taken. Though the cost is quite high, it only has to be met once a year, and there is a built-in guarantee of reaching a receptive market.

TV and radio advertising is expensive (particularly the former). If funds were available a short series of 'spots' for a heritage centre might attract extra visitors.

In any form of paid advertising it is important to establish a distinctive (but not gimmicky) house style and to write appealing copy which includes all the necessary information about charges, location and opening hours (if applicable).

(c) Promotion (free publicity)

For voluntary organisations free publicity offers the best prospects, and it is still very useful for other organisations which can afford paid publicity. The Press and local radio are usually very helpful provided some kind of 'story' is on offer; while guidebook writers and the like are under a moral obligation to give their readers reliable and up-to-date information, so will be glad to hear of new facilities.

Other media Each interpretive facility should include publicity for any others already in operation. Thus if a trail has been published, it should be publicised when (say) a mini heritage centre is provided. Apart from anything else the content of the facilities should feature cross-references, so that visitors who have enjoyed the mini heritage centre can be encouraged to enlarge their new knowledge by following the trail.

Street plans are available for most towns. Publishers should be asked to pinpoint larger interpretive facilities in future editions.

Town guides are a valuable source of publicity; publishers should be asked to take account of any interpretive facilities. In practice the editorial copy is often supplied by the local authority and the first approach should therefore be to the authority's chief executive, information officer or clerk (in the case of a parish or town council).

Tourist leaflets are issued mostly by the National and Regional Tourist Boards and local authorities and advice on town guides also applies to these.

Guidebooks and annuals are another important source of free publicity. As soon as facilities have been provided a letter should be sent to the publishers, preferably containing a draft amendment of the established text for the town or village concerned. All the relevant titles should be tracked down through libraries and bookshops and the opportunity may sometimes be taken of drawing publishers' attention to other omissions or inaccuracies. However it is unwise to adopt a querulous approach or to be so carried away by local patriotism as to demand an unreasonable amount of space.

Special visits are an excellent way of sustaining interest. Leading figures from outside the area can be invited to see or use the interpretive facilities and the Press and local radio invited to meet them. Alternatively (though rather less effectively), in the case of local weeklies, a report can be supplied to the news editor. Among those worth inviting are Government

Ministers, Tourist Board staff, senior academics, and persons with some special association with the area (the American or Australian descendant of some 19th-century emigrant, it may be, or the grandson of an architect, builder or industrialist who helped shape an area).

Special displays are another good means of renewing interest in established facilities. The centenary of the completion of a Victorian church, the 50th anniversary of the opening of a local school, or the 25th anniversary of the establishment of a new factory are all suitable occasions if the buildings concerned are already featured in (say) a community biography or wallsheet. Possible locations for such a display are libraries, community centres, adult education centres and the windows of empty shops. A small opening ceremony should be arranged and the Press and local radio invited.

Souvenirs are not free publicity in that they involve a capital outlay. However in the long term, provided they are well chosen and actively marketed, they are 'better than free' since they yield a profit and will encourage further use of the facilities. The range of possibilities is large and the minimum capital outlay (for 500 picture postcards or ballpoint pens) quite small—not more than £15 or so. Profits can be ploughed back to extend the range and increase the ultimate return. The sales aim should be high volume rather than high unit-cost and this needs to be borne in mind when ordering and distributing souvenirs. Material such as picture postcards, slides, tea towels and reproductions of old prints, maps and posters can often fulfil an interpretive function in themselves, so supplementing the facilities already available. Advice about sources of supply is given in Appendix 3, p 124.

Unusual feature of an exhibition to commemorate the centenary of Nottingham's Castle Museum was this fibreglass reproduction of an 11th century tympanum from a local church.

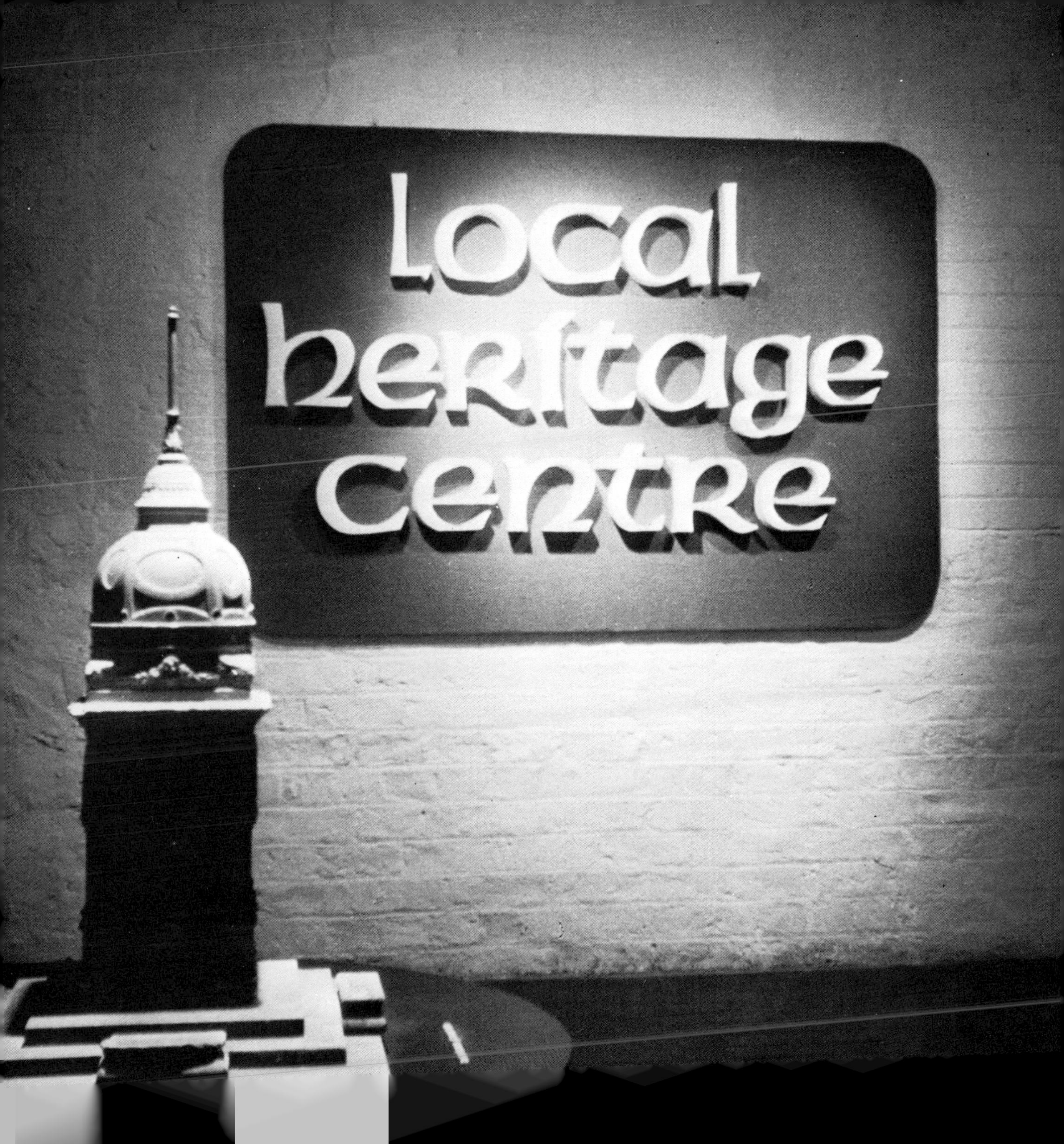
Local
heritage
centre

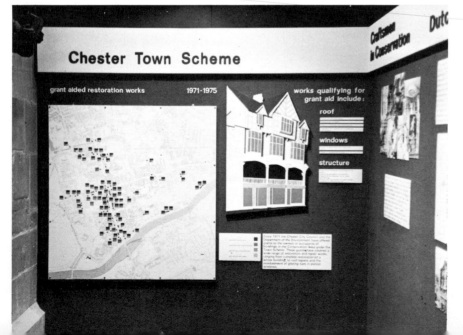

BRITAIN'S FIRST HERITAGE CENTRE

*Opened in June 1975, **Chester's Heritage Centre** is housed in the redundant church of St Mary, Bridge Street (above left), which is well-placed at the end of one of the famous Rows. After briefly tracing the history of the city, the displays created by the City Planning Department (left and above right) illustrate how with the aid of a special conservation rate and Government grants many historic buildings have been restored in recent years.*

Media in Detail

In this chapter more detailed advice is given on each of the media identified earlier (pp 38-39). Even when a particular medium has already been selected, it may be helpful to read the whole chapter, as some of the advice on one medium may also be helpful on others. More detailed information on capital and (when appropriate) maintenance costs is given in Appendix 2, p 115.

DISPLAY MEDIA

Except in the case of heritage centres (1), where more detailed treatment is necessary, advice is given successively on:

The application of each medium
Suitable locations
The technique involved
The likely cost
Presentation

(1) Heritage Centre

Concept and examples Of all the media for urban interpretation, the heritage centre is the most ambitious, for it amounts to a permanent exhibition with the evolution of a whole community as its theme. To serve its purpose properly, it needs a wide range of displays, full-time staff, and probably a building of its own.

The concept was introduced in Britain, where it has been pioneered, as part of the European Architectural Heritage Year campaign in 1975. By the end of 1978 nine heritage centres had been opened and since any organisation contemplating a similar venture would be well advised to visit at least two of these, a full and up-to-date list is enclosed as a loose sheet with this book. Further copies are available free of charge from the Civic Trust, 17, Carlton House Terrace, London SW1Y 5AW on receipt of a large stamped addressed envelope.

Capital costs and maintenance Even under the most favourable circumstances (free use of an existing building which requires a bare minimum of restoration and conversion, with a volunteer design team and staff) the capital cost is unlikely to be less than £12,500, and annual outgoings less than £3,000, at September 1978 prices. Where a suitable building has to be bought, restored and converted, and where volunteers are not available to design displays and serve as staff, both figures will be much higher—perhaps between £50,000 and £200,000 by way of outlay, and £12,000 by way of annual outgoings. These estimates may have to be adjusted to allow for inflation.

Space required The first requirement for a Heritage Centre is a large display area covering probably at least 2,000 sq ft (50 × 40ft) in aggregate. It need not take the form of a single room or hall of this size and indeed since to make the best use of the space it will have to be sub-divided, there may be some advantage in using a building where accommodation is already in the form of rooms.

The approximate display areas of the first four heritage centres are:

Centre	Display Area (sq ft)	Equivalent to space (ft)	Population
Chester	2,100	50×42	61,000
Faversham	2,950	50×59	15,000
*Pendle	2,350	50×47	86,000
York	4,750	50×95	107,000

* From 1980 the display area will be increased to 3,550 sq ft (equivalent to a space 50×71 ft). The population given is that of the whole Borough of Pendle, which the centre is intended to serve. It is situated in Barrowford (population 4,000) which is close to Nelson (33,000). The other main town in the borough is Colne.

The building For obvious reasons a Heritage Centre needs to be in or near the town or city centre. Usually it will be cheaper to convert an existing building than to construct a new one. If the building is listed and/or in a conservation area, it will probably be eligible for grant-aid from at least one source (see 'A Civic Trust Guide to Grants and Loans available for Conservation': this applies to England and Wales, and similar information for Scotland is available from the Scottish Civic Trust). Another good reason for converting existing buildings is that they are often of intrinsic architectural or historic interest (whether listed or not) and can themselves be 'on display' as part of the Centre which they house. This implies that

(continued on page 68)

Ashford Heritage Centre, in Kent, opened in 1978, is run in association with a teachers' centre. Displays (left), created at modest cost as a live project by a nearby College of Art, are housed (far left) in a property of 16th/19th century origin.

Border Warfare Centre, opened in 1978, occupies a disused barracks gymnasium (far left) in Berwick-upon-Tweed. Provided by the Department of the Environment, this permanent exhibition explains in detail how border fortifications reflect Anglo-Scottish relations and the evolution of firearms (left).

Durham Heritage Centre, administered by an ad hoc trust, is to be housed in the redundant church of St Mary-le-Bow (far left), in the shadow of the Cathedral. Until permanent displays are installed, the church (with its fine furnishings) (left) serves as a centre for temporary exhibitions on city and county.

Oldham's Local Interest Centre is housed in an 1867 Friends' meeting house (right) which was converted for its new use by the borough council in 1972. Changing displays on the area's development (far right) are complemented by a large local resource centre offering information on both past and present.

Pendle Heritage Centre opened in 1977 with the support of Nelson and Colne College of Further Education. An old farmhouse (right) has been adapted to accommodate displays (far right) illustrating the district's social and economic evolution.

Perth's Tourist Information Centre also houses an exhibition to introduce visitors to the city. The circular building (right) was built as a waterworks in 1832 and full advantage has been taken of its shape to create a panorama of displays round a central viewing deck (far right).

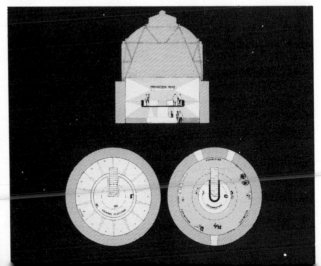

Private enterprise *created the Landmark Visitor Centre in Stirling, seen* (left) *from the Castle. A derelict hotel has been converted to provide exhibition space, an audio-visual theatre and a bookshop* (above).

The Broadland Conservation Centre at Ranworth, Norfolk (left) *is the work of the* **Norfolk Naturalists Trust**. *Unusually, but appropriately, the structure is a floating one, specially built for the purpose. Traditional reed thatch, grown locally, was used for the roof, and a special display* (above) *describes the techniques involved.*

Near Seaford an 18th-century barn (right) has been converted by **East Sussex County Council** to accommodate an interpretive centre for the Seven Sisters Country Park. Inside (above) care has been taken not to instal furnishings or equipment which would detract from the building's intrinsic character.

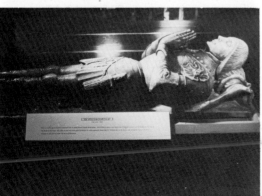

The Battle of Bosworth Field (1485) is the theme of a permanent exhibition mounted by **Leicestershire County Council** in former farm buildings (above) close to the battlefield site. Well-designed graphic displays (left, above) put the Battle in its historical context, while the spirit of the period is evoked by such three-dimensional features as an effigy (left, below) of a knight in armour—a replica of a church monument.

(continued from page 63)

restoration and conversion should be carried out thoughtfully, and by no means always with the object of recreating a building in its 'original' form. For example if a 17th-century building sports later accretions which are not wholly at odds with the spirit of the original work and reflect changes in its function, they should probably be retained (and explained) rather than removed.

Planning permission will be required for change of use. Listed building consent or planning permission (as appropriate) will be needed for major alterations (and listed building consent even for minor alterations to Grade I or II* buildings).

Of the first four Heritage Centres two (Chester and York) were housed in redundant churches, one (Faversham) in a redundant pub, and one (Pendle) in a former farmhouse now belonging to the Borough Council. Particularly if the purchaser is 'non-commercial' and has an educational use in mind some good bargains may be struck. York City Council paid the nominal sum of 5p for the medieval church of St Mary Castlegate which houses the York Centre, while the Fleur de Lis in Faversham was acquired by the Faversham Society from the brewers at the favourable price (1970) of £6,500. Neither building was badly decayed, but both still required extensive restoration.

For a local amenity society ownership of a Heritage Centre carries with it important fringe benefits. It offers a 'presence' in the heart of the community; the accommodation can probably be organised to provide rooms for meetings, storage and office purposes; and if the building is suitable it can provide a 'shop window' which if not used as such or to afford a foretaste of the Heritage Centre can be used for displays on topical planning issues.

Sales facilities It is essential to include a sales area within the Heritage Centre. This can either be incorporated in the ticket 'kiosk' at the entrance (if the entrance also serves as the exit) or it can be a larger, separate area. The more space that can be allocated, the better, as sales of local-interest publications, etc. can be an important source of income which can help offset running costs. Layout needs to be designed to deter shop-lifting. Rather than putting multiple copies of expensive books on display, for example, it may be best to show only a sample copy, keeping the main stock behind the counter. Advice about picture postcards and other products suitable for sale in a Heritage Centre is given in Appendix 3, p 124.

Other ancillary accommodation required in any event will include toilets, storage space, a small workshop area for running repairs to displays and equipment, and probably a small kitchen/staff-room.

Acquiring a building Even a comparatively small Heritage Centre (like Faversham) will cost a lot of money. How can it all be found by a voluntary organisation?

It is not impossible. The first problem may be to raise the money for purchase of the premises. There are at least three ways of surmounting this first hurdle—usually the most daunting:

(1) Do not buy a building but find one whose owners will offer a long lease at a peppercorn rent. This may not be as difficult as it sounds if there is a 'white elephant' property for which its owners have no use in the foreseeable future. Often as a result of local government re-organisation or the abandonment of redevelopment or road-building schemes local authorities themselves own such buildings. Listed buildings are often suitable candidates, if only because their demolition would be hotly resisted (by the society amongst others!) and the range of alternative uses to which they can be put is limited.

(2) Find a building whose owners (as in the case of St Mary Castlegate in York—see above) are willing to sell for a nominal sum. Again this is most likely to be a 'white elephant' property and listed.

(3) Raise a loan from the bank for the purchase-price and persuade the District Council to guarantee it (unless the society itself has sufficient funds to provide security). This means that if the society fails to repay the loan within a specified period (say three years) the building will become the property of the Council. For ideas on means of repaying the loan, see below.

Courses (3) and possibly (1) will involve the society obtaining financial assistance (of one kind or another) from the District Council. Some societies may feel this could effectively inhibit their right to take issue with the Council over other matters—e.g. development control. It depends on the relationship already obtaining between society and Council. If this is one of mutual respect, it is unlikely that any difficulties will arise.

Making plans and money-saving The society's next job is to draw up preliminary plans for the purpose of fund-raising. These must include estimates (as realistic as possible) of the cost of restoration, conversion, equipment and displays. The advice of an architect must be obtained on the first two elements and may well be helpful on the third and fourth.

It may be possible to reduce the cost of restoration and conversion by using society volunteers for some of the work but unless the society is *sure* it can rely on this and can identify an 'Hon. Clerk of Works' with the necessary expertise and the charisma to inspire the team it may be best to discount the possibility. If volunteers are not available when the time comes the scheme could be in jeopardy. Alternatively it may be possible to obtain assistance from the Manpower Services Commission; from the Chief Probation Officer in the area through the 'Community Service' scheme for adult offenders; from the British Trust for Conservation Volunteers (England and Wales: Zoological Gardens, Regent's Park, London NW1 4RY; Scotland: 70 Main Street, Doune, Perthshire*; or possibly in some cases from major local armed services establishments through the 'Military Aid to the Civil Community' scheme operated by the Ministry of Defence. Even if assistance is available from such sources a society will be expected to find at least a few volunteers of its own. For the purposes of fund-raising, however, it is best to assume that all building work will have to be undertaken by a contractor using his usual labour force.

Equipment includes panels and cases, lighting and projectors (if an audio-visual display is incorporated). If the panels and cases are specially designed it may be possible to save money by getting society volunteers to make them.

Three-dimensional material will be needed to relieve the monotony of two-dimensional displays. Some of this may take the form of specially built models or dioramas but the bulk is likely to consist of relevant artefacts. There should be little difficulty about obtaining examples of, for example, present-day building materials or products with a local provenance but for 'bygones', unless the society has its own museum collection, it will have to seek the co-operation of a local museum.

The curator will probably impose stringent security requirements which it is in the society's own interest to meet. Exhibits do not necessarily have to be sealed behind glass but they do need to be protected from theft and deterioration through sunlight or excessive handling. They must also be mounted or secured in such a way that no harm is done to them.

In the absence of a local museum the society may want to take the opportunity of starting its own collection but before doing so it should consult the curators of existing museums in the neighbourhood. Under no circumstances should a collection be started unless the society can reasonably expect that it will be properly stored and conserved, and on this score helpful advice may be obtained from Area Museums Services.

---

*The British Trust for Conservation Volunteers requires organisations using the services of its volunteers to meet their travelling expenses and also to make a payment of £1.50 per volunteer per day.

Though the society *must* provide a brief, will probably be responsible for some research and 'raw materials' (in the form of photographs, maps etc.) and may well provide a scriptwriter, the overall treatments needs professional expertise unlikely to be available 'voluntarily' within the society. The architect for the conversion may be able to supply this, or the society may commission a designer experienced in museum and/or exhibition work. A third possibility (which could save a substantial sum) is to invite the graphic design department of a nearby College of Art to carry out the work as a 'live project'.

As soon as preliminary plans have been completed and costed, the society should produce a feasibility study containing full details of the proposals for use when it seeks grants from public sources. This should explain among other things *why* the town or city is considered suitable for a Heritage Centre and *how* running costs will be met (see below).

Fund-raising General advice on this has already been given (p 42.) In the case of a heritage centre the society will probably want to begin by launching a public appeal locally. Apart from bringing in money, this helps to stimulate interest and may also encourage the gift of material suitable for use in the centre. A well-designed appeal leaflet (incorporating a tear-off donation slip) is essential, as is an effective launch. If the society is registered as a charity (as it should be, anyway), it can solicit covenanted subscriptions on which income tax can be reclaimed.

If the society gains possession of the premises before conversion and if they are suitable and in a good enough state of repair one good way of raising money is to open them as a charity shop. The society must of course be registered as a charity and it may require planning permission for change of use if the premises have not been used for retail purposes before. A sign inside the shop should make clear what its purpose is. If such a shop is opened there is no reason why the society should not also take the opportunity of starting to sell publications of local interest. There is a 50% mark-up (33⅓% discount) on books, and careful selection of titles combined with good stocks of the best-selling ones can help yield a useful profit. The shop will be manned by volunteers, of course, and though in the long term these will probably not be difficult to find it may be best to begin by opening only two or three days a week.

Grants from various sources will augment the society's own appeal. Any Carnegie United Kingdom Trust grant (see p 45) can provide only a smallish fraction of what is needed, so approaches will be needed to several other sources. On sources of official grants for the restoration and conversion of

Fleur de Lis Heritage Centre (left), *in one of the main shopping streets of Faversham, Kent, is run voluntarily by the town's local amenity society. Opened in March 1977 in a redundant pub, the Centre features displays designed to appeal both to residents and to visitors. After a chronological introduction to the town's housing from the 13th century to the present day (right) Faversham's evolution is outlined theme by theme (far right).*

a suitable building the Civic Trust's 'Guide to Gants and Loans Available for Conservation' and the Scottish Civic Trust's 'Guide to Conservation Grants in Scotland' give comprehensive information. Other than the Carnegie United Kingdom Trust there are no specific sources of grant for the heritage centre 'hardware' (equipment and displays) but approaches are worth making to any of the sources of grant aid listed on pp 42-46.

Running costs Once a Heritage Centre is established, what are its running costs and how can they be met? This depends on considerations such as those of size and staffing. Allowance has to be made for heating, lighting, insurance, advertising, cleaning, building maintenance, possibly rates* and (ultimately) renewal or replacement of displays. The costs are hardly likely to be less than £3,000 a year at least.

Allowance may also have to be made for staffing costs. However it may be possible to avoid these by manning the

Centre voluntarily. At first sight it may sound a tall order to find enough volunteers for this purpose—at least two will be required whenever the Centre is open—but any lively, average-sized society should have little difficulty. It will help if the premises have already been in temporary use (e.g. as a charity shop) before conversion, as a team of volunteers will already be in being.

Towards running costs the society may once again have to seek financial assistance from the local authorities. There is nothing wrong in this since the society has provided the area with a useful cultural, educational and tourist facility which it would otherwise lack—and has almost certainly done so at less cost to the ratepayer than would have been the case had the job been done by the local authority.

However it is better to be self-sufficient, or at least as self-sufficient as possible. The first, and main, source of income will be admission charges. When national and most municipal museums and art galleries are open to the public free of charge, it may go slightly against the grain to levy admission charges. However the fact remains that all but a handful of would-be visitors will be well able to afford them,

---

*Any registered charity enjoys 50% rate relief as of right. All or part of the remaining 50% may also be waived at the discretion of the local authority. No relief is available from water or drainage rates.

that in any event half-price concessions can be made for those likely to be less well-off (children, students and pensioners), that many people value more what they have to pay for (and therefore will make more effort to get their money's worth), and that the payment of an admission charge is a practical way of eliminating most of the 'undesirable' users who sometimes make a nuisance of themselves in free museums and galleries.

The level of charges needs to be carefully considered. If it is pitched too high, visitors may be discouraged; if too low, it may reduce takings severely without leading to any significant increase in attendance. There are two important considerations. In many cases visitors will come in family groups of, say, two parents and two children: charges which are high will seem even higher—and perhaps prohibitive—when father or mother has to fork out for '2 adults and 2 halves'. On the other hand if the Centre is good and there is nothing else like it in the area (almost certainly true) there is no point in undervaluing it. The 'cut-price' technique can be carried too far, and will be counter-productive if people feel that what is on offer is *too* cheap. 'It can't be that good: it's only 5p to go in, and 2½p for children. Makes you wonder why they bother taking any

money anyway.' Quite. Bearing in mind that (at the time of writing) adult admission to many major attractions such as stately homes costs about £1, it would not be too much to expect visitors to a heritage centre to pay between 30p and 60p each, depending on the facilities provided.

Running costs are pertinent—very pertinent. If they are £3,000 a year (for example) a quick calculation shows that to raise this the Centre needs to attract attendances of . . .

```
15,000 visitors at 20p  (50 a day on six-day opening) or
12,000 visitors at 25p  (40 a day on six-day opening) or
10,000 visitors at 30p  (33 a day on six-day opening) or
 8,500 visitors at 35p  (28 a day on six-day opening) or
 7,500 visitors at 40p  (25 a day on six-day opening)
```

15,000 may be a reasonable target for a Heritage Centre in a pedigree historic town already popular with visitors, while even 7,500 may be a challenge in a town off the beaten tourist track.

These are rough figures for purposes of illustration only. Detailed calculations would make allowance for the fact that a fair proportion of visitors, as children, students or pensioners, would be entitled to half-price admission.

They would also take into account that if there is a good bookshop in the Centre this will provide useful revenue and reduce the number of admissions required to break even. It is an immense advantage if customers can gain admission to the bookshop without having to pay to get into the Centre, and this can be achieved by siting it at the entrance or exit, the exit being preferable for visitors, who will be more disposed to buy after their visit than before it. Casual purchases are then possible and are likely (if the Centre is centrally sited) to account for as much as 50% of publications sales. Even with very little sales space (about 100 sq ft) but with careful choice of titles it is possible to achieve a turnover of at least £2,000 p.a., yielding a gross margin of around £700 p.a. With double the space it should be possible at least to triple the turnover. The necessary paperwork should not take longer than three or four hours a week, and in a voluntary organisation it should not be too difficult to find someone to take it on. The main overheads (other than those for the premises) are postage and stationery, and these are unlikely to amount to more than £50 a year.

Most publishers offer 33⅓ or 35 per cent discount. If adequate references are furnished, they will readily open an account.

Some offer free point-of-sale publicity material or even display stands, and these can be very helpful.

The best-selling titles are likely to be:

— *Those published by the sponsors of the Centre and related to its themes (though not necessarily directly to any specific display);*
— *Those on the particular community and county or region– particularly those from the smaller publishers which are difficult to find in ordinary bookshops;*
— *Those on general themes likely to interest visitors–again particularly from smaller publishers.*

Particularly in smaller communities it is vital not to trespass on the established territory of bookshops whose owners have to sell to make a living, but if stock is chosen on the basis described this is unlikely to happen. Selection of titles will always be a matter of trial and error in the sense that some will sell more slowly than others, but few books in the categories described will fail to sell at all. Since higher turnover means higher margins, there may be a temptation to phase out slower-selling titles but in bookshops which are also open to the general public this may prove a mistake because the fact

that they are readily available may build up customer loyalty and result in increased sales of *all* titles. If there is a local demand, and no-one else is meeting it, it will probably be worthwhile to cater for special interests related but not necessarily central to the purposes of the Centre—for example, transport history, wild life and industrial archaeology. Here again it is important to concentrate on titles which are not generally available in ordinary bookshops.

Books may be displayed conventionally, i.e. with the spines only on view and all stock in the sales area. Sometimes however it is better to display only single copies, with the front covers flat on inclined shelves. This drastically reduces the range of possible titles but it shows books off to better advantage, reduces the risk of damage through books being squeezed back between others on the shelves, and makes it easier to detect shoplifting. It presupposes that at least two copies of each title will be available (one on show and one for sale) but in any event once ready-selling titles have been identified it is wise always to hold at least three or four copies of each.

Picture postcards and souvenirs should also be on sale in a Heritage Centre bookshop. Advice about these is given in Appendix 3, p 124.

The number of visitors to a Heritage Centre can be increased by offering reduced rates for parties. If a society can also offer guided tours (see pp 101-105) of the area into the bargain, this will make the proposition even more attractive.

Members of the Society should enjoy the privilege of free admission to the Centre. Any small loss which results is likely to be outweighed by the fact that with a little encouragement they can be persuaded to make repeated visits, bringing their friends—who will pay in the normal way.

During the autumn and winter (when heating and lighting are most costly) a Heritage Centre will tend to attract fewer adult visitors and it will be advisable to boost attendance by attracting school parties. Liaison should be established with education authorities (county councils or in inner London the ILEA) and their advice sought about ways in which the Centre can serve the needs of schoolchildren. For example it is essential to provide teachers with briefing material *before* the visits and the children with brief notes and probably project sheets during them. These can be produced quite cheaply on

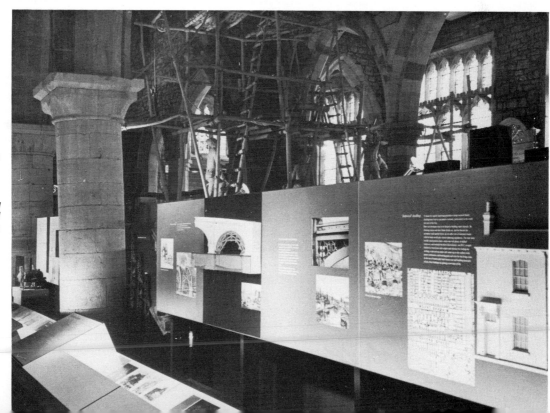

York's Heritage Centre, opened in 1975, is the most ambitious so far. Known as 'The York Story' (far left) and housed in a redundant church close to the famous Castle Museum, it was inspired by the city's Civic Trust. Dominating the nave is a near-life-size model (left) of medieval craftsmen at work. Recapturing important trends and events in York's long history are other imaginative and colourful displays (right).

a duplicator or by offset-litho. It helps if the Centre has a room where children can gather for discussion and project-work after they have seen over it. Some school parties prove a bit unruly but this can usually be avoided by insisting on prior bookings and a reasonably high teacher/pupil ratio. It must be made clear to teachers that a visit to the Heritage Centre is not just a 'jaunt'. Equally the Society must put itself out to make sure that the children are welcomed and made to feel at home.

Particularly if ancillary facilities such as a discussion room, projection equipment and project sheets can be made available, a Heritage Centre is likely also to fulfil the function of an Urban Studies Centre. The development of such Centres has been pioneered by the Town and Country Planning Association (17 Carlton House Terrace, London, SW1Y 5AS) who will be pleased to supply advice and information.

Promotion A Heritage Centre needs to be advertised. Fortunately not all advertising has to be paid for. A top priority should be to arrange for inclusion of details in regional and national handbooks and directories where space is free. Examples are regional Tourist Board guides and 'Britain's Heritage' (published by the Automobile Association). A relent-

less campaign also needs to be waged with the publishers or editors of established guidebooks to ensure that when the next edition is produced there is a (free) editorial mention of the Centre. If funds permit it is well worth placing one or two small paid advertisements in key publications with established markets—such as the 'Museums and Galleries Yearbook' and the regional Tourist Board guide. A small 'campaign' of this kind might cost about £150 and would probably more than cover its cost.

Handbills and posters need to be printed and distributed to sympathetic outlets for free display, e.g. libraries, schools, information bureaux, council offices, local history societies and other local amenity societies.

As the owners of stately homes know very well it is also possible to advertise facilities—and be paid for doing so! Ballpoint pens, badges, car stickers and even T-shirts, all carrying suitable messages or slogans, are only some of the things which can be sold to visitors.

Presentation Treatment of a Heritage Centre may be chronological, or thematic, or a mixture of both. The disadvantage of a pure chronological treatment is that the displays have

Ironbridge Gorge Visitor Centre is intended as an introduction to the area's rich industrial heritage. A disused warehouse (left) has been skilfully adapted to accommodate a series of evocative displays, including an impression (far right) of a typical local home of 60 years ago. Even views from windows (right, below) are captioned, and for visitors who want to find out more a wide selection of publications is available (right, above).

to be studied in exactly the right order and in full, or the visitor may lose his historical bearings. There is also a risk that visitors will lose the thread anyway by shunning periods they find difficult, though this should not happen if the displays are sufficiently lively.

A hybrid treatment is probably best. Introductory displays about the settlements's physical setting can be followed by a sequence summing up its history, wherever possible by reference to exact features and buildings. Thereafter the area's heritage can be illustrated by reference to such themes as:

A roof over your head (dwellings)
Building materials, traditions and techniques
Shopping
Market, fairs and trade
Industries (individually if necessary)
Public services (water supply, fire protection, police etc)
Transport (by individual modes if necessary)
Education
Social welfare (care of the poor, the sick and the aged)

Spiritual life
Local government
Farming (if appropriate)
Traditions and folklore
Important events (local disasters and triumphs)
Recreation and leisure
Conservation and planning

This list is not exhaustive and other broad themes may be dictated by local considerations. Indeed the safest rule is to identify what are the *key* themes for the particular community—those that shed most light on its present form, fabric and life—and then concentrate on these.

Captions and commentary must be crisply written, free of unexplained jargon, and accurate. Though the subject matter is parochial *they* must *not* be. The local information they impart must be related, wherever possible, to some *national* reference point which will be of interest to most visitors even if not all are already aware of it. If the reason why a new factory was built was to cater for a national market that was expanding dramatically at the time, the fact should be stated. If some local riots occurred as a result of a national slump in demand for farm produce, this should be mentioned. It may even be worth including an 'extraneous' illustration or two to make the point that unrest was not confined to one particular area.

Three of the existing Heritage Centres feature an audio-visual programme—i.e. an automatic slide presentation with synchronised commentary recorded on cassette. This does not mean all Heritage Centres have to have audio-visuals, but the medium is undoubtedly useful to introduce (or sum up) what is on show or to cover an extra topic or two. It has a number of other advantages, too. It is the cheapest way of showing photographs in colour (display-sized colour prints are very expensive). It is flexible: individual slides can be changed when required, or more than one programme can be shown. Above all, it saves space, since a whole series of views can be shown in the same place. Fuller advice is given in the section (4) on audio-visuals below.

A common view is that if captions and commentary are long-winded people will not read them in full. In consequence many exhibitions feature captions so terse that the visitor's curiosity is left unsatisfied. Experience suggests that it is a bad mistake to under-estimate the visitor's intelligence and that a caption of ten or even twenty lines will be read if it is relevant, informative and well written. In other words, the length should be dictated by the significant content of the illustration or object, not by arbitrary and possibly rather patronising assumptions about the level of visitor concentration. However, if there are more than a few long captions there may be a case for a series of parallel 'headline' captions. If there is, they should be given unity by running them at the same visual level throughout the displays. They should read consecutively and may help to give shape to the whole Centre.

Finally allowance should be made, if possible, for non-English speaking visitors. This is easier said than done. Clearly the displays themselves will not have room for bi- or tri-lingual captions and commentary. There may just be space for very short, almost perfunctory, captions in languages other than English but these on their own are not likely to prove very illuminating. The best solution is to give each display a number and then issue non-English speaking visitors with a free leaflet (duplicated would do) describing each one. It hardly needs saying that in most areas the two languages most likely to be in demand are French and German. Translation needs to be accurate and idiomatic and is best done by a native speaker. It should be checked, if possible, by someone else with a fluent command of the language. A leaflet in bastard-French or pidgin-German is worse than no leaflet at all.

The number of ways in which information can be communicated is limitless. Above. *A scale model in York's Heritage Centre recreates the bustle of the medieval butchers' quarter.* Below. *Life in an ordinary local home 60 years ago is vividly evoked by this sectional reconstruction at Ironbridge Gorge Visitor Centre.*

Above left. *This open-air model outside the City Museum enables the visitor to grasp the shape and size of Copenhagen as it was in 1500.* Above right. *Lending extra life to a Civil War display in the Richmondshire Museum is this life-size model of a combatant, clad in reproduction clothing and armour lent by the Sealed Knot.*

Below left. *Good photographs, skilfully masked and arranged, as at Ironbridge Gorge Visitor Centre, can make an arresting display.* Below right. *Simple but effective. In the Richmondshire Museum the names of the town's old pubs are linked by threads to their locations on a street-plan.*

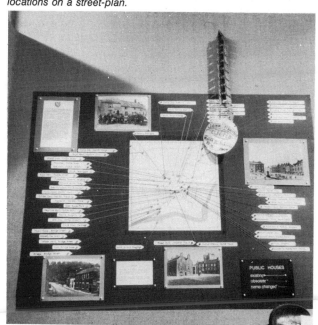

(2) Display Cases with periodically 'rotating' displays

Application, location and technique Fulfilling a similar function to a heritage centre but on a much smaller scale are sets of public display cases collectively illustrating and explaining the development of the local community. The cases are sited in places where people tend to throng—out of doors in squares, quays and market places, or indoors in such locations as railway stations, covered markets and civic centres. The displays are transferred in rotation from one case to another so that anyone 'following' the series can learn nearly as much as they would from a heritage centre. A street plan should be displayed in each case to pinpoint where the others are. When the displays have completed one circuit, they can be recirculated after any necessary updating.

More detailed advice is given below in section (5). Some of the advice on heritage centres (section (1), above) is also relevant. If a set of cases is to be provided, four is probably the minimum number to allow treatment of the most significant themes and to afford sufficient variety. To maintain interest the displays need to be 'rotated' every two or three months.

Cost The cost of four cases, inclusive of installation and displays, is likely to be at least £5,500.

The story of Lauderdale House, Highgate in London, is told in a display in the entrance hall (below). *Unusual but welcome feature of this Lincoln bank is an illustrated progress report on excavations nearby* (right).

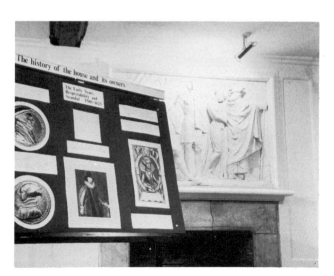

(3) Mini Heritage Centre

Application and location A good alternative to the fully-fledged Heritage Centre, particularly in smaller communities where the resources are never likely to be available for such an undertaking, is what might inelegantly be termed the Mini Heritage Centre. This is an attempt to deploy the same techniques but on a much smaller scale. The displays are housed not in a purpose-built or converted building but in *part* of an existing building to which the public have access and where space happens to be available. Examples of suitable buildings are town halls, information centres, railway stations and churches.

Churches (particularly parish churches of the established Churches or the Church in Wales, because they are most likely to be open to the public throughout the day) are specially appropriate locations. Almost always they are of architectural and/or historic interest themselves and are well-sited close to the centres of the communities they serve. Often suitable space will be available without causing overcrowding of the congregation. The displays should help attract more visitors and this should help any church which (like most) is hard-pressed to raise money for maintenance. Bearing this in mind, it may be as well in communities where there is more than one church open to the public to seek the agreement of the local

Council of Churches. They may wish to stipulate that any profits should be shared out between all churches rather than allocated to the one which has been selected to house the Mini Heritage Centre. Alternatively they may suggest that the displays should be shown at each church in turn for periods of (say) six months.

The great advantage of a parish church is that it usually constitutes in itself a kind of Heritage Centre in embryo. The building, the churchyard with its gravestones and the interior with its monuments, stained glass, fittings and furnishings are a living reflection of life and aspirations in the parish over a long period—often 400 years or more. Like a town itself, they can offer a fund of pleasure and insight—*if* visitors are given some necessary clues. Printed church guides, unfortunately, are not very good at giving clues, and many have nothing at all to say about 'minor' details such as tombs and stained glass.

Cost An area of at least 300 sq ft is needed and the cost is likely to be at least £2,000.

Presentation Wherever housed, a Mini Heritage Centre should take as its starting point the building which forms its setting. A ground-plan (chronological in the case of an old building which has developed organically), photographs or sketches of interesting details, illustrations of materials used for construction and fittings, and lucid text are essential.

The building can then be used as the reference point for the rest of the displays. How is it sited in relation to the rest of the community, and why? Are the building materials typical of the neighbourhood? What trends in the development of the area can be illustrated—in a church—by inscriptions on monuments, gravestones and stained glass? These are some of the questions to which the visitor will need to know the answer.

Design of a Mini Heritage Centre needs to be robust but simple and unassertive. There is much to be said for the use of a proprietary exhibition display system such as Marler Haley*, as units can be bought virtually 'off the shelf' and can be erected and dismantled easily—an important consideration if space may be needed temporarily for other purposes and if (as may be desirable) the Mini Heritage Centre is to be given an occasional showing elsewhere in the area.

Staffing It helps if a Mini Heritage Centre can be staffed, at least at times when business is briskest. For one thing, visitors may have enquiries. For another, it then becomes possible to sell publications, picture postcards and slides, which can yield a useful profit.

*Further details from Marler Haley Exposystems Ltd, 7b High Street, Barnet, Hertfordshire.

(4) Audio-Visual

Application and location As well as usually forming part of Heritage Centres, audio-visuals can also be provided independently elsewhere. For example, one on the architecture or evolution of an area could be provided in a museum, town hall, information bureau.

Technique and cost The technical sophistication of audio-visuals varies. At one end of the scale is a single projector with a maximum capacity of 80 slides; at the other, a triple-screen presentation with a battery of six projectors (three pairs, one of each pair 'dissolving' into the other) and a maximum of 480 slides. In each case back-projection is likely to be used, with the pictures being thrown onto a translucent screen from within a booth. Apart from projection equipment, a robust mains cassette recorder/player and a unit to 'pulse' the tape for slide changes will be needed.

Triple-screen audio visual at Chester Heritage Centre requires a bank of six projectors, one of each pair 'dissolving' into the other.

Nottingham Castle set on fire during the 1831 Reform Bill riots: one large, hand-painted transparency 'dissolved' into another at a special exhibition held in the Castle in 1978.

The projector generally used for audio-visuals is a Kodak Carousel S-AV 2000 (cost about £225) with a wide-angle (non standard) 28mm or 35mm lens (cost about £100). If there is space to construct a booth of above-average depth (i.e. over about 5′ it may be possible to save money by using a 70/120mm zoom lens (£40) at its widest angle (70mm). A suitable cassette recorder/player, incorporating a pulsing unit, costs around £200. Also required if all 80 slides in each magazine are not used may be a device to return the programme to its beginning. However this is expensive and with simpler audio-visuals it may be better to do this manually. Access to the projector booth should be fast and easy, particularly if only one or two staff are on duty. Otherwise the replacement of bulbs and any necessary minor adjustments will be difficult and time-consuming.

With a single projector there is a blank screen between changes and for an effective audio-visual the minimum requirement is a pair of projectors 'dissolving' into one another on a single screen. Since a standby projector is needed this means the minimum cost of equipment is in the region of £1,175. The standby projector however need not be fitted with an expensive wide-angle lens, as lenses are interchangeable. It can be fitted with a standard 85mm or 100mm lens (£20), thus saving about £80. The standby can then be used for normal (forward projection) purposes when required. Lamps can be replaced without changing projectors. Their life can be much extended by using the lower of the two power settings, as this impairs the brilliancy of the image very little.

For most interpretive work likely to be undertaken by voluntary organisations a two-projector single screen presentation is probably best. More ambitious schemes involve a bigger outlay, more risk of breakdown, and higher maintenance costs. Unless very skilfully devised, double and triple screen systems also carry with them the risk of confusing the viewer with too many pictures. However, if 'before' and 'after' scenes comprise an important part of a programme a double screen presentation is essential.

Instead of using slides and projectors, programmes can be transferred to film or video cassettes. There may be less risk of breakdown, but the process can be more expensive and if video cassettes are used the 'flickering screen' effect can be irritating to the eye and detract from the programme's impact.

Presentation Programmes should not be too long. It is not only that there is a limit to what people can absorb but also that if programmes are too long (more than 20 minutes) fewer people will have a chance of seeing them. In most cases quite a short programme, lasting about 10 minutes, will be sufficient to introduce viewers to a particular theme. The simpler and more direct the approach, at least for a general introduction to a subject or area, the better. It is tempting to lace the programme with artistic mannerisms (flashbacks to the remarks of 18th or 19th century travellers for example) but the only result may be to confuse and alienate viewers. On the other hand it would be a pity not to exploit some of the near-cinematic effects that can be achieved, the most apposite perhaps being views of a single building taken from successively closer vantage-points, or a series of views down a particularly interesting street.

The greatest care needs to be taken with the selection of a speaker to record the commentary. He or she needs to have a voice free of mannerism or affectation, and the ability to use inflections to bring life to the script. However strong local loyalties may be, experience suggest that regional accents are best avoided, as strangers can find them difficult to follow.

Slides need to be specially taken and the same film 'stock' should be used for all of them as different makes of film have quite different colour balances and variations can be surprisingly obtrusive and irritating. Since slides tend to fade in constant use, each view should be taken in duplicate or even triplicate so that replacements are readily available. The cost of materials (including glass mounts to protect the slides from dust) is likely to be about £75 but of course much more will have to be paid if the work is commissioned.

Though a top-grade camera is not essential, it helps; what is more important is good pictorial technique, and some advice on this is included in Appendix 4, p. 128. If 35mm film is used, as normally it will be, the slides may be of vertical or horizontal format but never of *both* in one presentation. Except perhaps for some special themes the horizontal format is the better one, though it does make it difficult to illustrate such 'vertical' subjects as towers and spires to the best advantage. There is something to be said, therefore, for the use of square-format slides. Within the constraints of the standard 2″ mount, these can be taken on 'rapid' film to yield images 24mm square, on 126 film to yield ones 28mm square, or on 127 film to yield ones 40mm square. A word of warning, however: cameras for the 24mm and 40mm format are no longer made, while few of those for the 28mm one are capable of work of the necessary technical standard.

Servicing Projectors need to be regularly serviced. Since repairs and maintenance are costly a local society may find it worthwhile where the county council has a supplies department to seek registration as a customer. The Local Authorities (Goods and Services) Act 1970 enables non-commercial organisations to obtain supplies and services through county supplies departments and if a society is considered eligible for registration it may be able to save money not only on projector repairs and maintenance but also on a wide range of other goods and services.

(5) Display Case

Application, technique and cost One of the best means of promoting interest in the local heritage is to provide a display in a special showcase, which can be sited either out of doors in a big urban space such as a market place or indoors in such locations as covered markets, shopping centres, civic centres and railway stations.

The technique, though rewarding, is relatively new in this country. A combination of graphic and three-dimensional material is used either to provide an introduction to the whole area (in which case the facilities need to be sited centrally) or to interpret the immediate location. Alternatively, if sufficient funds are available a single centrally-situated showcase may be used for a *succession* of displays about the area. The best thing is then to plan a two- or three-year programme, allowing each display to be on show for two or three months.

Suitable cases (costing about £1,250) are those sometimes installed by local authorities or advertising contractors in open-air shopping precincts. Most of these are robustly but simply designed and will blend in with any environment. If cases are custom-built, extravagant or 'rustic' designs should be eschewed at all costs, if only because maintenance costs and the risk of vandalism will be increased and an assertive design may distract attention from the content and detract from the immediate setting. Professional advice will almost certainly be needed to ensure not only a high standard of aesthetic design but also good weathering properties, resistance to vandalism, and the provision of the concealed ventilation needed to avoid condensation and the damaging effects this can have on displays and artefacts. Manufacture of metal cases is probably best carried out by a shop fitting firm.

Location Planning permission and/or consent of owners of land or buildings will be required. Great care needs to be taken with the siting of cases. To minimise the risk of vandalism they need to be in prominent locations, but if at all possible they should also be sited to escape the worst extremes of weather.

Designed as an information kiosk but capable of being used as an outdoor display case is this unit made by Urban Enviroscape Ltd.

Tree-cover, if available, will afford protection from the elements for case and user, but the risk of soiling by birds needs to be borne in mind. It is not advisable to site cases on grassed areas, for though these may be dry in summer they may be muddy in winter and the turf will soon be worn away. They must not obstruct pedestrian circulation, nor in pedestrian areas access by emergency vehicles, and the setting must be taken fully into account. Thoughtlessly and unsympathetically sited, a case can be at least as intrusive as an ill-located traffic sign. In any location armour-plateglass or polycarbonate glazing is essential, and if the case is exposed to daylight ultra-violet protection will also be required.

Presentation For the displays it is best to adopt a fairly 'popular' approach, seeking first to arrest attention and then to maintain it against the competition from neighbouring window displays. It helps that three-dimensional objects—building and other local products, models, bygones and the like—can be featured. However, if bygones or other museum-worthy exhibits are incorporated the greatest care must be taken of them, and the advice of a professional curator sought about mounting techniques. Under *no* circumstances should historic documents (including manuscripts, and old photographs) be subjected to prolonged daylight, let alone sunlight.

Though in theory there is plenty of space, it soon goes if displays are confined to the floor of the case. Somehow use has to be made of its height, too. It may be possible to do this by inserting a vertical 'divider' for two-thirds the length of the case and using this for backcloth or title on either side. Glass shelves on metal brackets could also be used, as they are in shop windows. Objects can also be suspended on strong nylon thread from the roof of the case. If a succession of displays is planned, a consistent 'house-style' should be adopted—and also a modular form, so that if the series is repeated and modifications are needed they can be made without disturbing the overall concept.

A simple street plan of the locality should always be included and if there are complementary facilities—another display-case or a trail (see below), for example—the opportunity of referring to them must not be missed. Equally, if relevant publications are available in a nearby shop, this should be mentioned—and it would be no bad thing to make sure there are at least a few interesting picture postcards which can be bought as permanent mementos.

In some cases where the amount of material exceeds the space available, it may be possible to make arrangements with a nearby building society for the use of its window space for an overflow or supplementary display. Building societies are particularly helpful in this kind of way because they have little to put in their windows and a mini-exhibition never fails to attract goodwill and investors! Alternatively, a vacant shop can be used. If this can be staffed (by volunteers in the case of a local society) publications can be sold and visitors' questions answered. It can also be used for recruiting purposes and in appropriate cases for the collection of museum material.

Outdoor display cases used for advertising in Wakefield (left) and Stockholm (right). Those in Wakefield were purpose-built in 1977 by a local shopfitting firm at a cost of £1,600 each (inclusive of installation).

Vantage point key (in English, French and German) overlooking the site of the Battle of Hastings: screenprinted and stove-enamelled on an aluminium panel by a local signmaker for East Sussex County Council, this cost £400 in 1977.

(6) Vantage Point Key

Application and location Vantage point keys are already popular in the countryside. Sited on bluffs and hilltops they identify distant landmarks that can be seen on a clear day—e.g. other peaks or ranges, rivers, lakes and conspicuous buildings. However there is no reason why such keys should not be installed in commanding positions with good views in towns and cities. Here buildings and streets are likely to be more prominent, and a key to the bird's eye view that is obtained can reveal a good deal about the way the community has evolved, especially if not far away there is an accompanying display board of the kind described below.

Presentation and cost Keys are best engraved on metal and set on a simple, stout plinth of brick or stone. The cost is likely to be at least £300. By definition they will be in exposed positions and design and workmanship need to take this into account. It is worth bearing in mind, too, that the 'key-plate' may need to be updated in the future if there are important changes in the view. For ease in comparison with the view the key needs to be set at an angle of about 15° from the horizontal. For adults keys need to be about one metre above ground level, but as this is too high for children it is a good idea

to provide a shallow step about 20cm high at the foot. The key needs to be large enough to allow three or four people to look at it at once and if there are interesting views in more than one direction a group of two or three keys may be provided.

If possible, it helps if some overlap can be included in each.

As an elaborate, expensive but effective variation on this theme, the *camera obscura* is worth mentioning. This is an optical device, rather like a periscope, by means of which a small audience in a darkened room below the top of a tower see projected down onto a horizontal 'screen' at table-height the image of the view from the top as it actually is. The basic principle is the same as that of a conventional, photographic camera, except that there is no film, the image is a continuous one, and the device is on a much, much larger scale. Since the lens can usually be revolved throughout the whole of a 360° horizontal field, visitors can study the view segment by segment. This is not the kind of facility which can be left unattended and the usual arrangement is for the custodian who operates the camera to explain to visitors the significance of the various views. Among examples are the Clifton Observatory and Camera Obscura in Bristol (opened in 1828); the Great Union Camera Obscura at Douglas, Isle of Man (built some time between 1882 and 1889); the camera obscura, housed in an old windmill tower, at Dumfries Museum (opened in 1836); and—perhaps best known of all—the Outlook Tower in Castlehill, Edinburgh (opened probably in 1855–56). Elsewhere—in museums for example—the same principle is sometimes illustrated by a primitive rig consisting of a window totally blacked-out except for one tiny round opening between about ¼″ and 1″ in diameter. If a small enclosure round the inside of the window is sealed off from extraneous light and a white screen provided opposite the opening, an inverted image of the outside view can be seen. The smaller the opening, the sharper (but dimmer) the image. If a lens is substituted for the simple opening, the image becomes crisper.

A similar principle is used in the *camera lucida,* which was the precursor of the (photographic) camera. Until the advent of photography (and indeed for some decades after it) this device was used by artists to enable them to draw objects in correct perspective. The uncanny realism of some early 19th century engravings of street architecture owes a great deal to the *camera lucida.*

Camera obscura, Dumfries: visitors see a bird's-eye-view of the town and its setting as they actually are.

(7) Display Board

Application, cost, location and technique An outdoor display board serves a similar purpose to an outdoor display case. It costs a good deal less—as little as £150 if only materials have to be paid for—but of course it offers no scope for the use of three-dimensional material. This is not necessarily a disadvantage, for in some locations such as a small village square, the entrance to a park, or a windswept wharf a showcase would be inappropriate—whereas a display board might not be.

In many communities it may well be worthwhile providing a series of display boards at key sites. These could be planned in sequence to supplement information given in a trail (15) or sound trail (14). Alternatively they could be erected instead of plaques on a signed trail (9). Such boards are probably the best way of encouraging people to join a trail.

A simple street-plan of the locality should normally be featured on every display board, and if more than one is erected, the position of the others should be indicated on the plan. There may also be an opportunity to direct users to any local museum which includes material relevant to the locality.

Much of the advice given about display cases (5) applies to display boards. They need to be simply and robustly designed, and craftsman-built of durable materials. They should be sited prominently enough to minimise the risk of vandalism but sympathetically enough to avoid visual intrusion. Planning permission and/or the consent of owners or land or buildings will be required.

Presentation Though only two-dimensional material can be used, a display board's large flat surface gives it one advantage over a case. It is possible to feature such graphic material as large-scale street plans with illustrations of interesting structures superimposed in the right place or long 'ribbon' views of street elevations.

Overall design of the display needs to be carefully thought out. An attempt to include too much material will result in a 'busy' effect, which will probably bore people: on the other hand if content is too thin and lay-out too stark they may give the board only a passing glance. At all events, though a board should not be crammed with material, it is important not to leave so much blank space that there is an irresistible temptation to graffiti-writers.

Great care needs to be taken to see that the display is weatherproof. If there is a good local signwriter with real artistic ability the whole of the board—both text and illustrations—may be hand-painted, with the finished work

The first and last of a continuous sequence of 12 display boards at Darlington (Bank Top) Station. Designers were members of staff at Hartlepool College of Art and help was given by BR and the NUR.

varnished but otherwise uprotected. The board needs to be properly prepared (with primer and undercoat) and preferably not sited where it will be exposed to too much sunlight—otherwise peeling and fading will soon set in. Alternatively the display will have to be glazed not with glass, but with polycarbonate, which is virtually indestructible. It is a good deal more expensive, but well worth the extra outlay. To minimise fading, particularly if photographic material is used, one of the transparent films which resist ultra-violet light should be stuck on the inner surface of the glazing. The The biggest problem with a glazed display, however, is not fading but condensation, which can quickly ruin material of any kind. There are various ways of avoiding this. The first of course is to ensure that there is at least an inch between the inner surface of the glazing and the display material. This will not prevent condensation, but it will reduce the damage. Good ventilation is important but needs to be concealed to overcome weather and vandalism problems. Alternatively silica gel crystals may be used.

All these approaches assume that artwork is produced in conventional form, on card or board, and then displayed behind the glazing. However other techniques are possible, though some may be more expensive. The Norfolk Heritage Project (see p. 92) for example has evolved a system—which seems more or less foolproof—whereby the text is photographically enlarged and then silk screened directly onto the back of the polycarbonate sheet. Another method is to get printed matter laminated in transparent film and then glued to an aluminium sheet. The lamination is cheap and waterproof, but not scratch-proof. If the board has a shiny surface (of whatever kind), it may be possible to avoid distracting reflections, or glare, by canting it at a slight angle.

A third technique, quite widely used, is to screen-print artwork (using a transparent film positive) onto a special paper which is impregnated with melamine resin and then sealed with protective layers which are also resin-impregnated. The display panel is then bonded together with wood or aluminium by heat and pressure to form a stiff laminate. One advantage of this technique is that aerosol paints can be easily removed. Panels of this type can be made to order by such firms as Formica Ltd (Coast Road, North Shields, Tyne and Wear, NE29 8RE—North Shields 75566) and Perstorp Warerite Ltd (Aycliffe Industrial Estate, Darlington, Co Durham, DL5 6AN—Aycliffe 315141).

Outdoor display boards vary in style and treatment. A standard-model TIP (p 87) in Worcester (top left) contrasts with a custom-built board (centre left) in Durham (p 87). Providing detailed information about particular sites are a triangular unit in Chester (bottom left); simple post-mounted boards in Norwich (above left), Nottingham (above right) and Philadelphia (below left); and a four-sided display in Boston (Mass.) (below right).

If a site merits a display board, it will probably be worthwhile (i.e. profitable) to publish a picture postcard or two of the locality and arrange for a nearby shopkeeper to hold stocks. In this case details should be included in the board's text. Further advice on picture postcards is given in Appendix 3, p 124. If the display board incorporates suitable line-drawings, as it may well do, these too can be reproduced and sold. A local printer may well be prepared to produce an initial run of 1,000 for about £20.

Alternatively, and more ambitiously, if several display boards are provided, a set of Heritage Guide Cards (see section (11) below) can be published to elaborate upon the information they give and serve as a permanent reminder of what has been seen.

Tourist Information Points A variant of the outside display board is the Tourist Information Point (TIP)—a feature whose design has been pioneered by the English and Scottish Tourist Boards. The aim is to welcome visitors and give them their bearings. In England, the first were installed in 1976 and by August 1978 there were 130 in all. Among places where they have been provided are Cheltenham, Corbridge, Felixstowe, Lewes, Middlesbrough, Preston, Stockton and a number of regional airports. They are best sited at such arrival points as car parks, bus stations and railway stations and at key points along major pedestrian routes. In most towns, even the smallest if they are of above-average interest, there will be scope for a number of TIPs though a single one will be better than none at all.

Three standard models, all carefully designed to enhance rather than detract from their setting, are available. The first (TIP/1) is single-sided and can be wall- or column-mounted. The second (TIP/2) is double-sided and mounted on a mild steel tube column. The third (TIP/3) is three-sided and also column-mounted. Aluminium and alloy extrusions are used for the body, with perspex glazing.

Though at £260 the three-sided TIP is the most costly and needs a site where users will not obstruct other pedestrians, it is the most effective since it can include the most information. An illuminated version is available at £314 and the supporting column (£36). In England the, installation and artwork is extra in each case, layout of each panel must follow a formula from the ETB. Design and execution can be undertaken either locally or through the ETB. Panels commissioned through the ETB cost £140 each. This means that if the panels are produced in this way the total cost of a three-sided TIP (exclusive of installation) is £716, or £770 if illuminated.

Comparable costs for a single-sided TIP are £234 and for a double-sided one £376. A 25% discount off all these prices is given if the TIP fully conforms to the ETB's requirements.

Normally one panel of a three-sided TIP carries national information (together with a directional indication of the local TIC), one local and one regional. The national panel includes a large route-planning map of England and information about TIC's; the local panel features a street-plan (with the position of the TIP marked 'You Are Here'), an introduction to the locality, details of places to visit within it, and possibly photographs or drawings of local scenes; and the regional panel contains rather similar information about the surrounding area. Thus at least two panels can be interpretive and all three can be if (as in some cases) a national panel is not included and there are two local or regional ones instead. However if the national panel is omitted one panel must contain a short reference to the national network of TICs.

So far most TIPs have been provided, and the costs met, by local authorities and other public agencies. However there is no reason why voluntary organisations should not take similar initiatives. In certain circumstances in England, provided that the TIP is used purely for interpretive purposes, such organisations might obtain an ETB 'Special Promotions' grant through the relevant regional tourist board (cf p 44); and local amenity societies could apply for grant of up to 50% of cost under the 1978/81 Heritage Interpretation Programme (see p 45). Further information about standard-model TIPs is available, in the first instance, from the regional tourist boards (cf p 44). Alternatively, the manufacturers, Urbis Enviroscape Ltd, of 95 Walton Street, London SW3 (01-589 6279) or the ETB's Networking Section, of 4 Grosvenor Gardens, London SW1W 0DU (01-730 9842) will be able to provide details. Since arrangements outside England are different, societies in Scotland, Wales, Northern Ireland, the Isle of Man and the Channel Islands are advised to get in touch direct with Urbis Enviroscape Ltd.

Similar in concept, but rather different in appearance and presentation to standard-model TIPs are the four interpretive boards installed in 1978 at key locations in the city of Durham. Provided as part of a co-ordinated scheme to improve tourist signing, these are large single-sided glazed display boards mounted in a hardwood frame. Featuring prominently is a large street plan incorporating sketches of interesting buildings and views. The whole scheme benefitted from a 50% 'Special Promotions' grant and further details are available from the City Planning Officer.

As far as possible advice is given in the same order for each medium. After details of *application* and *technique,* at least one *example* is usually described. Information about likely *outlay* and (where appropriate) *revenue* is given, and finally advice about *promotion* and (where appropriate) *marketing.*

(8) Community Biography

Application and Technique This is an attempt to tell the life-story of a place from the time of its first settlement to today. It is the published equivalent of a Heritage Centre and much of the advice given about such Centres (pp 63-77) applies to community biographies. In particular the community biography should explain how the area's evolution has shaped its present form. Maps, drawings and photographs will all be essential if the biography is to tell its story lucidly.

The aim should not be to compile an exhaustive account—which in most cases would involve years of research—but to identify the main strands in the community's development, describe them and explain how they have been interwoven to influence the area's fabric and life. The book may be a community biography in more senses then one—different chapters may be assigned to different authors, so that the work as a whole becomes a community effort.

Narrative and analysis form the backbone of a community biography. However the book's impact will be increased if it can include passages with a more immediate, documentary appeal. If they refer to key events or trends, contemporary documents or newspaper reports are often work reprinting in full. Likewise if the society has taken an active interest in oral history, transcripts of interviews can be published. These may vary from eye-witness accounts of particular events to reminiscences of school-days or reflections on a lifetime's changes in local industry or agriculture. If there is a member skilful enough, it can be well worthwhile to incorporate a chapter or two of historical reconstruction—for example an account by an imaginary eye-witness of the building of a local canal. It needs to be made clear at the start of any such passage that it *is* a reconstruction and a note of the historical evidence on which it is based should be given at the end. Like any life-history, a community biography should include a good index and an indication of the source of the material on which it is based.

Example A splendid example of a community biography is *Market Drayton: A Town and its People,* published in 1978 by the Drayton Civic Society and obtainable, price £3.10 post paid, from the Society at The Red House, Wollerton, Market Drayton, Shropshire.

More than 60 local people were involved in the production of this 110-page book, which in the words of the editor, 'faithfully records the leisurely evolution of a certain type of English settlement'. Drayton is a typical small town with all the commercial, industrial and social attributes that give such communities an importance out of proportion to their size. The first chapter outlines the town's history: 15 others take as their themes such topics as architecture; the street market; churches, chapels and clergy; schools and schooling; sport and recreation; local newspapers; and public houses. Particularly welcome—and interesting—are chapters on post-war housing, the town's changing social structure and the evolution of local government (title: 'Are You Being Represented?')

The book is handsomely designed, lavishly illustrated with photographs old and new, and well produced. Three of the chapters are 'team efforts' contributed with their teachers' assistance by children in local primary and junior schools. Design was undertaken—very successfully—as a student project in the graphic design department of a nearby polytechnic. These features could usefully be adopted elsewhere.

The book also makes clear how crucial is the editor's role. Great care must be taken, as it has been in this case, to select a representative cross-section of themes and then identify suitable contributors. To avoid wasteful overlap, clear briefs must be given; and when the contributions arrive, they must be integrated to form a coherent whole without detracting from their individual flavour.

Outlay and revenue Bearing in mind in particular the need to include plenty of illustrative material, offset-litho is the most economical printing technique. If a local society is publishing the biography, it can save money by finding members to do the 'type-setting' on electric typewriters, produce artwork and do 'paste-ups' for the printers.

Production costs will still be quite heavy and, as an illustration, 1,000 copies of a 96-page biography in A5 format with 50 illustrations would cost about £1,250. However the bigger the investment, the larger the potential dividend and if all 1,000 copies are sold (half by direct sales at a cover price of £2.25 and half at £1.50—allowing for the usual trade discount of 33⅓%—to local retailers) a profit of £625 should accrue. This can be ploughed back to finance a reprint, another publication or some environmental improvement work.

Promotion and marketing The market for books of this kind is now quite buoyant but promotion will still be needed. A press notice must be issued and review copies distributed. There will probably also be a case for holding a modest reception to launch the biography. This need not involve a heavy outlay but it is a useful opportunity for the local Press and prospective purchasers to meet the authors and perhaps also representatives of some of the interests—such as long-established local businesses—which feature in the book.

Efforts should be made to obtain as many outlets as possible. Some private traders, particularly if they are members of the society, may be prepared to waive trade discount; but *never* presume upon goodwill of this kind. Discount should always be offered, even if it is refused.

Other considerations The vast majority of new books are now assigned International Standard Book Numbers. The job is usually done by the publishers, so that the number can be printed in the specified places (e.g. on the back of the title page). Each publisher is given a list of consecutive numbers to assign one by one. Any organisation which publishes books or booklets ought to take advantage of this system, further details of which can be obtained from the Standard Book Numbering Agency Ltd, 12 Dyott Street, London, WC1A 1DF.

Copies of the biography should be sent free of charge (as required by law) to the national 'copyright' libraries—the British Library, the National Library of Wales, the Scottish National Library, the Bodleian Library (Oxford), the Cambridge University Library and the Library of Trinity College, Dublin. The copy for the British Library should be sent to the Copyright Receipt Office, British Library, Store Street, London WC1E 7DG. Postage can be saved by sending the copies for the other five libraries to the Copyright Agent, Mr. A T Smail, 100 Euston Street, London NW1 2HQ. Sending a copy to the British Library ensures that the publication will be listed in the British National Bibliography and this can result in useful orders. Notification of publication should also be sent to 'The Bookseller', 12 Dyott Street, London WC1A 1DF, which lists all new books free of charge in its weekly issues.

(9) Listening Posts

Applications and technique The listening post is a new medium which has been developed in conjunction with the Countryside Commission (England) by Rediffusion Reditronics Ltd. The basic concept is a self-contained cartridge tape playing device which is audibly unobtrusive since the sound is piped to the ear by a special tube costing only a few pence which can be sold, hired and recycled, or given away. There are a pair of outlets on each side of the post and the user presses a button to start the tape which can last up to 10

Listening posts can be installed unobtrusively in the open air or under cover, as here at Ironbridge close to the bridge (above), *near a Telford tollhouse* (centre) *and in the Tar Tunnel* (below).

minutes though 2 minutes is probably the optimum length if congestion is to be avoided. Ruggedly built, the listening post is weather resistant and designed to be immune from vandalism, theft and hygiene problems. Access for maintenance is easy with a special tool provided, and as the post is only about a metre high, 300mm across and 150mm deep it is reasonably unobtrusive.

The standard model is powered by its own rechargeable battery but one variation provides for a remote D.C. supply. Another provides for remote supply of the audio signal from a cartridge player located elsewhere. In sheltered sites outdoors, and indoors, a small wall unit (comprising only a row of four outlets and a push-button) may be connected to a remote tape player. This version is so unobtrusive that it may require special signposting.

The script and recording are undertaken by the sponsoring organisation. As with a sound trail (14) three important advantages are that users can study what they see as they hear about it (instead of having to look at a leaflet or booklet); that the human voice can communicate emphasis or enthusiasm more effectively than the printed word; and that (within limits) a touch of drama and variety can be added by interpolating other voices—first-hand reminiscences or recordings of such documentary material as old newspaper reports.

Examples Because of the Countryside Commission's involvement with their development, most listening posts have so far been installed in rural situations. Among urban locations where the idea has been tried is Ironbridge, where a number of posts have been provided by Ironbridge Gorge Museum Trust.

In built-up areas sites in noisy streets should be avoided since the standard earpiece fits into one ear only. A double tube, for both ears, is available but costs twice as much. At the same time sites need to be prominent enough to attract users and to deter attempts at vandalism. For purposes of maintenance they need to be easily accessible.

Outlay and revenue Probably to offer users any worthwhile benefit at least four listening posts, at four different sites in an urban area, are required. The capital outlay for such an installation would be about £1,208, comprising £832 for posts, £108 for battery packs, £88 for a battery charger, £35 for cartridges and tape, £27 for a diagnostic unit (the posts are fitted with an 8-function diagnostic socket), and £100 for installation.

In order to advertise the facility handbills would have to be printed and £100 a year should be allowed for this. Other annual outgoings can only be estimated: insurance might cost £120, maintenance £293 (including the cost of listening tubes and earpieces sufficient for 5000 hirings a year), and depreciation £274 (50% per annum on batteries, 20% on other equipment). Total outgoings each year would then amount to £787.

If there were 5000 hirings a year at 25p a time, income would amount to £1250, yielding a net margin of £463.

Promotion and marketing The listening tubes must be available for hire at a suitable central point. If the sponsoring organisation has no permanently staffed premises of its own it should come to an arrangement with the tourist information centre, council offices, museum, bus enquiry office or a local shopkeeper.

The handbill should be available at the point of hire and also at hotels, libraries, the tourist information centre etc.

(10) Signed Trail

Application and technique This is a trail (see (15) below) where a printed leaflet or booklet is supplemented by informative plaques or other outdoor displays, such as display boards (7, above), at key points on the route. Alternatively or as well the trail may be signed by pavement markings, either stencilled on the footway or inlaid into it, using inset studs or specially cast paving slabs. The design of these should incorporate a direction arrow .

Detailed advice on informative plaques is given in Appendix 5 (p 133). One very important point is that in towns and villages with many listed buildings it would be visually disruptive to erect plaques on all, or most, simply to record that they are listed. Equally it could be dangerously misleading to erect plaques with inscriptions to this effect on just one or two of the listed buildings. It is best to avoid 'listed building' plaques altogether.

Though stencilled pavement markings are much cheaper to provide than inset studs or specially cast slabs, they suffer from the disadvantages that they require periodical repainting and that in all but the largest-scale environments they may prove unacceptably obtrusive, only adding to the unsightly array of white and yellow lines which already disfigure so many carriageways. Both kinds of marking are unnecessary where directions given in the printed trail are—as they should be—sufficiently clear.

Inset studs can also be useful to mark the precise sites (where reliably known) of vanished features such as market crosses, bull-rings and gallows. Similarly narrow strips of non-ferrous metal or strips of stone setts, can be inlaid in suitable locations

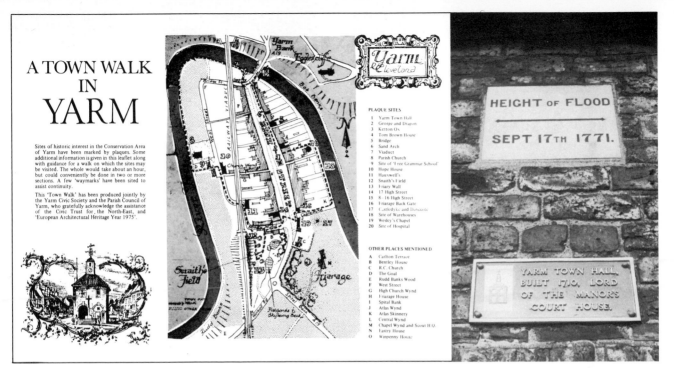

A TOWN WALK IN YARM

Sites of historic interest in the Conservation Area of Yarm have been marked by plaques. Some additional information is given in this leaflet along with guidance for a walk on which the sites may be visited. The whole would take about an hour, but could conveniently be done in two or more sections. A few 'waymarks' have been sited to assist continuity.

This 'Town Walk' has been produced jointly by the Yarm Civic Society and the Parish Council of Yarm, who gratefully acknowledge the assistance of the Civic Trust for the North-East, and 'European Architectural Heritage Year 1975'.

PLAQUE SITES

1. Yarm Town Hall
2. George and Dragon
3. Ketton Ox
4. Tom Brown House
5. Bridge
6. Sand Arch
7. Viaduct
8. Parish Church
9. Site of 'Free Grammar School'
10. Hope House
11. Hauxwell's
12. Snaith's Field
13. Friary Wall
14. 17 High Street
15. 8-16 High Street
16. Friarage Back Gate
17. Castledyke and Dovecote
18. Site of Warehouses
19. Wesley's Chapel
20. Site of Hospital

OTHER PLACES MENTIONED

A. Carlton Terrace
B. Bentley House
C. R.C. Church
D. The Goal
E. Rudd Banks Wood
F. West Street
G. High Church Wynd
H. Friarage House
I. Spital Bank
J. Atlas Wynd
K. Atlas Skinnery
L. Central Wynd
M. Chapel Wynd and Scout H.Q.
N. Eastry House
O. Winpenny House

HEIGHT OF FLOOD SEPT 17TH 1771.

YARM TOWN HALL BUILT 1710, LORD OF THE MANOR'S COURT HOUSE.

At Yarm in Cleveland the Civic Society and Parish Council combined forces to create a signed trail. Identifying each plaque on the trail is a symbol based on the Town Hall's distinctive silhouette.

to indicate the courses of underground streams, the sites of important buildings, or old parish boundaries. For a child it is a memorable experience to stand astride the Meridian line inset into the paving in this way in Greenwich. To this day, too, boundaries are quirky things, not without real social and/or economic significance, and many adults enjoy the experience of standing somewhere in what appears to be a homogeneous street, but with one foot in one parish, district or county and the other in another. If attention is then drawn to nearby buildings it will sometimes be noticed that their flank walls are askew, reflecting 'fossil' or living boundaries.

Examples A good example of a trail supplemented by informative plaques is that laid by Yarm Civic Society during European Architectural Heritage Year 1975. As the route lay within a non-outstanding conservation area, a small Heritage Year Grant was made towards the cost. Within similar areas in England 'Section 10' conservation grants continue to be available for this as well as other purposes considered conducive to their enhancement. Further details are available from the Civic Trust, which administers such grants on behalf of the Historic Buildings Council for England.

The Silver Jubilee Walkway created in London in 1977 exemplifies the other type of signed trail, where route advice in a published guide is reinforced by pavement markings. In this case the marking adopted was the special London Silver Jubilee emblem. Originally it was stencilled on the footway, but in 1978 when the Walkway was extended and made permanent arrangements were made for these markings to be progressively superseded by specially cast paving slabs incorporating the emblem.

Outlay and revenue The cost of a trail supplemented by informative plaques will probably be at least £700, allowing for the printing of 5,000 leaflets consisting of a single A4 sheet folded in three and the manufacture of 16 cast aluminium plaques. This estimate is based on the assumption that copy and artwork for the leaflet, and installation of the plaques, is undertaken on a voluntary basis. In other cases costs will be appreciably higher. Further information about the cost of plaques is given in Appendix 5 (p 133).

The cost of a trail supplemented by stencilled markings, inset studs, or cast paving slabs will vary according to length. As an illustration, the trails laid in the City of London during European Architectural Heritage Year 1975 required a total of 375 chrome-nickel studs, each 150mm in dimeter, laid at 15m intervals. They were obtained from H Johnson Foster Ltd, of Aizlewood Road, Sheffield S8 0YT at a cost of £1.65 each. Fixing costs £4 for each stud.

In course of time it may be possible to recover part or all of the cost of a signed trail, or even make a small profit, by the sale of trail leaflets. Relevant guidance is given later (see (15) below).

Promotion and marketing Advice is given below (15).

Other considerations It is important to note that under the Carnegie United Kingdom Trust's Heritage Interpretation Programme (see p 45) grants are *not* available for the erection of plaques unless they form an integral part of a signed trail.

(11) Heritage Guide Cards

Application and technique This is a new idea. Series of cards, with anything between 10 and 40 in a set, are produced to highlight different facets of an area's heritage—its industrial development or transport history, for example. The cards, well-printed on durable board, probably to A5 format, are on sale at or near each featured building at such outlets as shops, pubs and churches. They are available singly or in sets, the sets coming with a clear plastic wallet for which a charge may be made. In addition a 'book of the series' may be published to provide background information on each set.

The concept is an ingenious one. It appeals to the collecting instinct; it offers a 'branded' product of uniform quality and style; it is compact and handy; and it may be backed up by a 'book of the series'. Since the term 'heritage' need not be construed in a narrow sense, the technique is as valid in an industrial town as a pedigree historic one. The cards could be linked with *display boards* (see (7) above), an *explorer's kit* (see (13) below), a *conservation area guide* (see (12) below) or a *trail* (see (15) below), supplementing the information given in these. It is essential of course for each card to give publicity to the series as a whole and any supporting material.

Examples The idea has been pioneered by the current experimental 'Norfolk Heritage Project', which operates as a department of the county museums service, with the support of the Countryside Commission, Carnegie United Kingdom Trust and East Anglia Tourist Board. Series of cards, each series linked to a booklet, are being produced on such aspects

Some of the heritage guide cards produced for the Norfolk Heritage Project.

of the county as its scenery, transport systems, agriculture and industry.

The first series takes 'Water Transport' as its theme and consists of 32 cards (10p) each, a booklet (45p) and a wallet (25p) to hold both cards and booklet. These may be obtained from Norfolk Heritage, Beech House, Gressenhall, Dereham, Norfolk NR20 4DR (please add 15% for postage and packing). Cards and 28-page booklet are both to a common style and A5 format. Each card takes a particular site or building as its theme and includes about 600 words of text as well as photographs or drawings (often of a feature as it was in the past) and usually a plan or map. Complementing the cards— seen indeed as an essential part of the project—are on-site display panels (cf (7) above) containing about two or three hundred words selected from the text of the relevant card.

A similar initiative has been taken quite independently by the City of Rochester Society. A series of A5-sized 'heritage cards' is being published on such individual buildings of note as the Guildhall add Rochester Bridge. On the front of each is a sketch of the building, complemented by a 500-word text which continues overleaf. On the back is also an illustration of an interesting detail, a location plan, a brief bibliography and details (where appropriate) of opening time. All artwork and copy is provided by members. The cards are sold at 5p each and the main outlet is the city's tourist information centre. The initial print order was 1,000 of each. The unit cost worked out at 1.4p (1978) and the Society makes 2.1p profit on each card it sells to outlets at 3.5p.

Outlay and revenue Assuming that copy and artwork are produced by voluntary effort, the cost of 1,000 sets of 15 illustrated cards, printed offset-litho in two colours to an A5 format, with 1,000 clear plastic wallets, might be about £650. If all 1,000 are sold (half by direct sales at a cover price of £1.20 and half at 80p—allowing for the usual trade discount of 33⅓%—to local retailers) a profit of £350 should accrue. This can be re-used for further interpretive or environmental work.

Promotion and marketing The advice given above about community biographies (8) also applies to heritage guide cards.

(12) Conservation Area Guide

Application and technique There is immense scope here, particularly for local amenity societies. There are now nearly 5,000 conservation areas in the United Kingdom but though there is much public interest in them and most form coherent areas of great charm only a handful of guides to them have been published.

To justify its title a conservation area guide must include a trail (see (15) below). But the background will need to be filled in. The following are among the questions to be answered in the guide:

— What is a conservation area? (What are the legal provisions and what do they imply for owners, occupiers, and planning and highway authorities?)

— Why has this particular area been designated? (What are the characteristics that give it a special claim to conservation and enhancement?)

— How has it evolved? (What is its history—up to the present day?)

— Where does it need enhancing? (Where does it quality fall short, and why? What can be done to redeem any defects?)

— What policies has the local authority for the area? (For example does it operate a 'town scheme' jointly with the Historic Buildings Council to enable the owners of certain listed properties to benefit from repair grants which would not otherwise be available to them? In a town centre conservation area, does it have plans for the exclusion of through traffic? In an inner city district, is the conservation area also a general improvement area where housing and environmental improvement funds can be harnessed?)

In some conservation areas character is eroded by well-meaning but unidiomatic alterations such as the addition of bow windows to Victorian houses or the cladding of brick walls with artificial stone. The local planning authority can adopt control powers but these are time-consuming and in the long run better results are likely to be yielded by persuasion.

It is at least as important to offer positive advice—for example about the principles of external decoration and the importance of any distinctive local building materials and/or techniques. If a local society is responsible for the guide, it may be able to get help here from the local authority's conservation officer (or equivalent).

Particularly useful to those with property interests in the area will be an 'information panel' summarising the range of grants available from central and local Government; the names, addresses and telephone numbers of responsible local officials such as the conservation officer, environmental health officer and district highway engineer; and those of ward councillors and members of the conservation area advisory committee. If supplies of replacement materials such as natural stone or pantiles are hard to track down, it would be useful to include details of suppliers. A detailed description of some of the work involved in the production of a conservation area guide is given earlier (pp 49-54).

Outlay and revenue Assuming that copy and artwork are produced by voluntary effort, the cost of 5,000 copies of a 16-page conservation area guide with 12 illustrations printed offset-litho to an A5 format might be about £625.

If all 5,000 are sold (half by direct sales at a cover price of 25p and half at 16.7p—allowing for the usual trade discount of 33⅓%—to local retailers) a profit of about £400 would accrue. However it would be a pity not to issue the guide free to all owners and occupiers of property in the conservation area, and this will affect the budgeting.

Promotion and marketing The advice on trails (15) also applies to conservation area guides.

(13) Explorer's Kit

Application and technique An explorer's kit is similar to a trail (see (15) below) but produced in a different form and invites users to do their own detective work. It may also invite them to draw their own conclusions. The emphasis is often on 'before-and-after' comparisons. Corresponding to the seaman's charts, compass and plumb-line is a kit consisting of a basic route-plan supported by a sheet of notes and such documents as photographs old and new, maps old and new, tradesmen's letterheads, and press cuttings.

Keyed to the route-plan by numbers, the documents enable

A chronological sequence of views from the same standpoint can be included in an explorer's kit and users invited to form their own judgements about whether change has been for better or for worse: Oxford Street, London, at the corner of Edgware Road c 1912, c1960 and in 1978.

the explorer to draw his or her own conclusions about particular buildings and sites by studying what is there now in the light of information given in the kit. Careful selection of sites and documents is needed to ensure that recognition and comparison is not too difficult. For example if an old photograph is used to highlight the changes that have taken place since 1920 in a row of shops, at least one of them must not have been altered beyond recognition. If a pre-war map is included to illustrate how a street pattern has been affected by major redevelopment, two or three key features must still remain.

The sheet of notes can be either explanatory or provocative. An explanatory sheet points out changes and passes judgement on them. A provocative sheet also points out changes but invites the explorer to form his own judgement on them. He or she can be asked to 'score' each site (from −2, for 'much worse than it was', to +2, for 'much better than it was') and then tot up the figures to see whether in his or her view the whole area looks better or worse than it did (say) just before the War. Explorers can also be asked how they think sites or vistas which are obviously degraded might be improved—by tree planting? by redevelopment? by rehabilitation? and so on. The process of having to 'decide' between various alternatives will probably prompt them to apply the same technique elsewhere. If a local society is responsible for the kit, they can also be asked to participate in its work by posting their completed returns to the Hon Secretary, and the addition of an 'Any Other Comments' section may well produce useful feedback.

Outlay and revenue Thanks to offset-litho printing methods such kits need not be too expensive, particularly if in a voluntary organisation members can produce the necessary artwork. On this basis the cost of 1,000 kits (each consisting of 30 loose sheets of A4 format in a manilla wallet) might be about £600. If all 1,000 are sold (half by direct sales at a cover price of £1.20 and half at 80p—allowing for the usual trade discount of 33⅓%—to local retailers) a profit of about £400 would accrue.

Promotion and marketing The advice on community biographies (8) also applies to explorer's kits.

(14) Sound Trail

Application and technique. A sound trail is a trail (see (15) below) where the written word is replaced by the spoken one, recorded on cassette and reproduced on a hired player. Its advantage is that the human voice provides a personal element missing from the printed trail. It can also communi-

94

cate emphasis or enthusiasm more effectively—providing the narrator has the necessary skill to read the text as if it were *not* being read. A touch of drama (and variety) can also be added by interpolating other voices—first-hand reminiscences of a particular custom, event or building by older people, or recordings by other 'actors' of contemporary newspaper reports and other suitable source-material. Victorian journalists left no stone unturned to produce colourful copy and a reporter's account of a fire, a funeral or the opening of a factory hardly ever fails to conjure up an evocative scene. Equally they were meticulous about their reporting—*verbatim* and *in extenso*—of speeches and if it so happened that a Spurgeon or a Disraeli ever appeared at a hall on the route extracts will prove irresistible.

As with audio-visuals, so with sound trails: the greatest care needs to be taken with the selection of a narrator. He or she needs to have a voice free of mannerism or affectation, and the ability to use inflections to bring life to the script. However strong local loyalties may be, experience suggests that the best narrator may be someone with a 'BBC' accent. The same applies to any 'actors' needed to read documentary extracts. At the same time their voices should be easily distinguished from the narrator's.

For the recording of first-hand reminiscences some skill is needed. Subjects with strong regional accents may have to be asked to speak more slowly than usual, or there is a risk that strangers to the area will not understand a word they are saying. A lot depends on good interviewing technique. The art is to establish a rapport with the subject such that he or she keeps talking without the need for frequent prompting.

Some local amenity socieites and a few universities have already begun oral history programmes and if recordings are already available they will prove very useful. Equally work on a sound trail may serve as the cue for the commencement of such a programme—and very worthwhile it is likely to prove. It is not only that for vividness nothing can match the human voice. It is also that many people for whom it would be difficult or a chore to commit their reminiscences to writing will gladly record them; and that often while actually recording they will remember things they thought they had forgotten!

Experience suggests that 30 to 45 minutes is enough for the commentary on a sound trail of 1½ to 2 miles, which should begin and end at the same point. This implies the use of C60 or C90 cassettes, as the same trail is recorded on both sides and the cassette simply turned over on return by the hirer to save re-winding.

The trail should begin and end at some convenient central point where players and cassettes may be hired and which is open at least in the afternoons most days of the week. Unless an organisation has its own office, the best thing is to come to some arrangement with a friendly shopkeeper or obtain the co-operation of the local council offices, information bureau, museum or bus enquiry office.

A sound trail may be supplemented by a sequence of display boards (7).

To obviate the risk of loss through theft, a deposit may be required for the player and cassette. This can be either a cash sum or (perhaps more convenient for both parties) a document such as a Banker's Card or Passport. However as long as players rather than recorders are used it may be possible to operate without requiring a deposit—the less versatile machines are less vulnerable to theft. In any case machines can be prominently marked to deter theft and it may also help to house them in special brightly-coloured covers—which to a limited degree can also serve as a form of publicity for the trail. Earphones should be issued only if facilities are available for sterilising them after each hiring. It is best to assume that earphones will not be used and this implies that when recording the commentary care must be taken to ensure that playback cannot exceed the noise-level of ordinary speech.

Outlay and revenue. To launch a sound trail will probably cost just under £600. This allows for the purchase of 10 players and the necessary ancillary equipment but does not include any allowance for production and printing costs. Hire rates need to be fixed to cover initial costs, batteries and depreciation and should also allow a profit margin to the sponsor and commission to the hire-point operator.

Though the initial outlay is heavy, it is well worth investing in rechargeable (nickel-cadmium) batteries as running costs are lower than those of conventional cells and a regular recharging routine will ensure that players are never lent when batteries are on the point of going flat. Details of suppliers of such batteries can be supplied by the Civic Trust on request.

Promotion and marketing. Details of a sound trail should be advertised on a handbill available from information bureaux, hotels etc and conditions of hire should be specified. These will probably include requirements for return of the players and cassettes, details of excess charges if they are returned late, and a stipulation that if an instrument is lost or returned damaged, the hirer shall be liable to meet the full cost of replacement or repair. Hirers should also be reminded of these conditions when they borrow the players. If a sound trail is supplemented by a sequence of display boards, these can also be used to advertise it.

(15) Trail

Application and technique. Annotated tours round historic towns have been the stock-in-trade of guidebooks for many decades. However, the weakness of most has been that they take a blinkered look, ignoring all but the obvious landmarks and wallowing in colourful but all-too-often unsubstantiated associations of the 'Queen Elizabeth I slept here' variety. Often, too, they assume too much knowledge on the part of the reader ('note how the Perp. works shows lingering traces of the Dec.' or 'this was the home of the well-known painter Richmond').

Town or history trails, which began to appear in the United Kingdom in the 1960s, try by contrast to be broader and more explicit in their approach. An interesting feature is worth some space whether it originated in 1566 or 1966. If some church tracery is transitional in character, it helps to explain what are the characteristics of the twin ingredients and how they show in the particular window.

Examples. To date well over 500 town trails have been published in the United Kingdom, and this is one sphere in which local amenity societies have already made a substantial contribution. A list of some of the best trails is given in Appendix 6, (p135), so that readers who which to devise a trail can obtain copies of suitable examples. A comprehensive list of town trails in Britain was published in 1975, and revised in 1976, by the British Tourist Authority. Though now out of print and not to be re-issued, this may be available in local libraries. The Institution of Evironmental Sciences (14 Princes Gate, Hyde Park, London SW7 1PU) plans (1978) to publish a new and up-to-date list of town trails.

One trail or several? If trails are too long (over a couple of miles in a town), not many people will ever complete them, even though in theory they can break off and come back another day. In most towns, including some of the smallest, there is a strong case for devising at least three or four trails. The first should probably be an introductory one to whet the appetite:

---

*See also the advice given on pp 6-8; Brian Goodey, *Urban Walks and Town Trails: Origins, Principles and Sources,* Centre for Urban and Regional Studies, University of Brimingham, Selly Wick House, Selly Wick Road, Birmingham B29 7JF, £1.50 + postage; and *Make a Trail,* free from the National Council of Social Service, 26 Bedford Square, London WC1B 3HU, on receipt of a stamped addressed foolscap envelope.

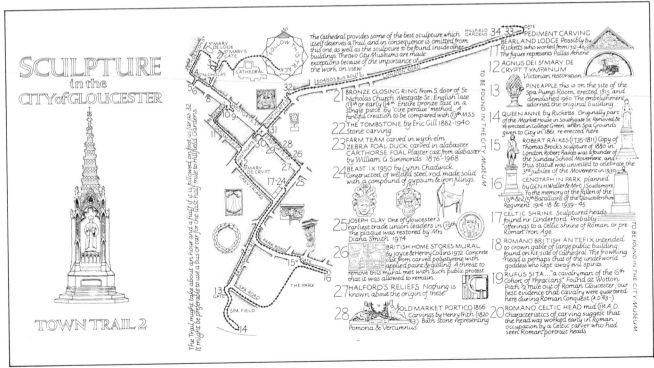

the others can interlock to cover the rest of the ground, perhaps in greater detail. If the trails are published separately, as they usually will be, each one needs to include a mention of the others, of course.

Theme If more than one trail is published, it may be a good idea to relate routes to subject-matter rather than area. 'Exploring Industrial Forchester', 'Riverside Forchester' or 'Victorian Forchester' may make a more appealing package than 'A Walk through Walton Ward'.

Format A popular format, at least for an introductory trail, is a single sheet of A4 folded in three to give a 'cover' and five 'pages'. This is easy to use and fits comfortably in a pocket or handbag. If more space is needed a single sheet of A3 can be folded in half and then in three to give a 'cover' and eleven 'pages'. Alternatively trails can be printed in booklet form. An A5 format (210mm x 148mm) is compact and quite convenient. For ease of reference pages should be clearly numbered. The price should be printed on the cover and the date of publication included. If the trail takes the form of a booklet it should be assigned an ISBN and copies sent to the 'Copyright' libraries (further information on these topics is given in section (8) above).

Text Jargon should be avoided but if it is essential for full enjoyment of a particular trail to use architectural or other technical terms they should be explained, perhaps if there are several of them in a short glossary, which may need to be illustrated. A common fault is to use without explaining them phrases which are well-understood locally but may be obscure to visitors—e.g. Hornton stone, mathematical tiles, vennel and so on. When the first draft is ready it is advisable to get it read by an outsider so that obscurities of this kind can be explained.

The trail is best preceded by a brief introduction to the area or theme. At the end it helps to include a panel of useful local information (about early closing and market days, and bus and rail services, for example) and a paragraph or two about the society itself. This is also the best place for 'credits' to author, illustrator and designer. A concise bibliography and notes on other places of interest in the vicinity may also be useful.

There is often a strong temptation just to pinpoint and describe (in isolation) the most obvious buildings of interest—but this should be avoided. A good trail also draws attention to a wide range of features that might otherwise escape notice—for example the way settlement patterns have been influenced by natural features; the way key buildings such as abbeys,

A theme trail – one of several produced by Gloucester Civic Trust. The handwritten text integrates well with the map and illustrations (left). Imaginative feature of Reigate Society's town trail is a map in the form of a bird's-eye-view. Every feature mentioned in the text is numbered and pinpointed (right).

REIGATE TOWN TRAIL

This trail is intended to be a guided walk of about 45 minutes through the oldest part of the town centre. It is not encyclopaedic, although we hope it includes all the main buildings of historic interest to be found on the route. There are of course many historic buildings in Reigate which are not on the route. We hope this trail will help you to discover and enjoy them too.

1   Old Town Hall
2   La Trobes, 4a High Street
3   Castle Grounds
4   Castle Keep Cottage
5   Castle Gateway
6   The Castle
7   32 High Street
8   42-50 High Street
9   53-53a High Street
10 The Bulls Head
11 65 High Street, The Pantry
12 The Red Cross
13 6 Slipshoe Street
14 10 Slipshoe Street, Old Sweep's House
15 20 Upper West Street
16 28 Upper West Street
17 Horse Trough
18 Ceylon Forge, 36 West Street
19 Old West Street House
20 Farley Cottage
21 Browne's Lodge, 22 West Street
22 31 West Street
23 The Blue Anchor
24 19 & 21 West Street
25 Priory Park Motors (Medieval Undercroft)
26 77a High Street
27 77 High Street
28 Geranium Cottage, 12 Park Lane
29 Priory Lodge Cottage, 7 Park Lane
30 Priory Park
31 The Priory
32 49-51 Bell Street
33 38 Bell Street
34 37-39 Bell Street
35 16 Bell Street
36 10-12 Bell Street
37 15 Bell Street
38 The White Hart Inn (Site of)

market houses and factories have helped to shape street patterns; vernacular building characteristics; floorscapes and rooflines; and building details which are interesting for their craftsmanship, innovative significance, or the insight they afford into social history. Remeber too that though in one area grey bricks, millstone grit or pantiles will seem perfectly ordinary because they are the common coinage of building in the locality, they may seem unusual, and therefore interesting, to a visitor from Cornwall or the Cotswolds, where materials are very different. It is also important to avoid the 'history-stops-at-1830' syndrome and to bear in mind that visitors may be as interested in good modern buildings as in 'period' ones.

Often arousing more spontaneous curiosity are buildings which have outlived their original purpose and been adapted for another—the corn exchange into a library at one end of the scale, the stables into a cottage at the other. As well as recording such changes and perhaps commenting on the success, or failure, of the conversion in architectural terms, a trail should explain what factors dictated it.

However, a trail need not be 100% exposition. At intervals when opportunities arise it may help to invite users to test their powers of observation. Take the case of a house, standing on a corner, which was once a pub. The text might say:

> 'At the next corner on the right is 223 Main Street, a showy Victorian building that looks for all the world like a pub. The reason for this is that until it was de-licensed in 1962 it was a pub. It has now been converted into a house, but its name survives in Crown Street on the corner of which it stands'.

It might be better to say:

> 'At the next corner on the right is 223 Main Street, a showy Victorian building that is now a private house but until 1962 served a different purpose. Look at the big wooden cellar flaps, the large decorative ground-glass windows on the ground floor, and the double entrance doors on the corner, and you will soon realise what it was. If you want to know what it was called, you need only look at the street nameplate on the side wall.'

If numbers of visitors from abroad warrant it, it may be worth considering the publication of at least one foreign-language version. Translation is best done by a national of the country concerned who is also reasonably fluent in English, but failing this a teacher in a local school may be able to help. In either case it helps if the translator is also an environmentalist, with a knowledge of any necessary technical terms. As professional translation fees are high, particularly for technical work, it is best to find a volunteer. If at all possible another volunteer should be found to check the work, as only the highest quality of translation is acceptable and unintentional errors can puzzle or mislead readers.

In the case of a booklet costs may be reduced by including a few advertisements. These have their own interest, particularly if illustrated, and if they are placed by builders, estate agents and the like may be useful to readers. There is a better chance of obtaining advertising revenue if the authors of the trail can suggest suitable copy related to the character of the contents.

Maps A street-plan, with the trail and any fixed stopping-points suitably indicated, is essential. A location plan also helps visitors gain their bearings, particularly if there are distant views from particular vantage-points. (It is surprising how even in towns which seem quite flat there are views from central points to distant landmarks such as hills, woods and church towers, and these are worthy of note—though often overlooked by local people).

In some cases it may be possible to use for the street-plan an extract from the 1:2500 (25″) or 1:10,000 (6″) Ordnance Survey plan, in which case the permission of the Director General will be required, and a royalty payable—unless the plan is out of copyright (i.e. more than 50 years old). If the plan is specially drawn it needs to be very clear and if possible to include details of useful amenities such as railway and bus stations, car parks, libraries, shopping streets and public conveniences. If the society has a skilful artist as a member it may be possible to produce a bird's-eye-view type of plan which features both the street-pattern and elevations of some or all of the buildings along the trail.

Illustrations are a great asset, almost to the point of being essential. They help to identify landmarks along the route, can be useful to highlight interesting features that are not very conspicuous, serve to spice the text, and are useful reminders of what has been seen. Good clear line drawings are probably best because they enable key characteristics to be stressed, and reproduce well on any quality of paper. If photographs are used, they need to be of good quality (see Appendix 4, p. 128).

Design should be clean and simple. A good idea is to have on the cover an illustration of a feature which epitomises the area or theme. If there are several different trails it can be helpful to print each one on different-coloured paper. It goes without saying that they should be produced to a common style and format. A good graphic designer is a great asset, but if funds are limited it may be worth approaching a local college of art to see if graphic design students may be willing to help.

Supplementary facilities A trail may be linked to a sequence of display boards (7) which can provide supplementary information 'on-site'. They can also encourage more people to join the trail itself.

Outlay Assuming that copy and artwork are produced without charge it should be possible to produce 5,000 copies of a modest trail (consisting of a single A4 sheet folded in three, with six illustrations, printed letterpress on coated paper) for about £300. If the trail is published by a local amenity society, part of the cost may be met by a grant from the Carnegie United Kingdom Trust (see p. 45), but the society will have to find the remainder. It can set about this in a number of ways:
— It may be sufficient to hold two or three small fund-raising events—at which the draft trail can be on display.
— If the trail is in booklet form costs will be higher (perhaps about £625 for 5,000 copies of a 16-page A5 booklet) and the society may want to augment its own resources by selling advertising space. Prospective advertisers such as local traders and industries will want to know what they are buying—i.e. how many copies are being printed, how they will be distributed, and what method of presentation is being used. It will often help if the society can suggest some suitable copy for each advertisement. Wherever possible this should relate to the content of the trail—and if it does, it can often be of considerable interest in its own right. Advertisements are best printed in separate panels or sections: if integrated with the text, they may prove too distracting.
— If one trail is priced to yield a profit (see *Distribution*), the revenue can be used to help finance another.
— In some cases an introductory trail in the form of a folded leaflet can double as a 'town brochure' designed to attract visitors. On the understanding that it can have whatever supplies it likes a local council may then be prepared to meet the entire cost, or a substantial part of it. One trail produced and seen through the press by a local society and financed by a district council is now in its 6th edition.

Distribution methods will vary according to whether the trail is sold or given away free. If it is given away:
— Make sure copies are always in good supply at such appropriate outlets as council offices, information bureaux, libraries, hotels, churches and bus and railway stations. It is an advantage if the society can offer 'help yourself' dispensers. Not much ingenuity is needed to fashion these from cardboard, hardboard or plywood, but they do need to be neatly designed and well finished.

— Though in principle it may also be a good idea to have copies available from outdoor dispensers where these can be under cover (e.g. under an awning or in an arcade), great care is needed to see that these are sited where they will not be too obtrusive or too much of a temptation to vandals. Careful thought also needs to be given to design and wording.
— Regional Tourist Boards may be pleased to take bulk stocks for distribution through their own Tourist Information Centres. Similarly the amenities or information officers of nearby local authorities may be prepared to arrange for copies to be available at the Tourist Information Centres for which they are responsible. Lists of addresses of Centres in their areas are available from Regional Tourist Boards.
— Copies should be available at all society functions.

Promotion and marketing If the trail is sold:
— The cover price should make allowance for *both* a trade discount to shops *and* a profit by the society. For example, if 5,000 leaflet-type trails cost £300, at a unit cost of 6p, the retail price might be 10p, allowing copies to be sold wholesale at 33⅓% discount (6.7p a copy). If half the copies are sold wholesale and half by direct sales, a profit of £116 will accrue.
— Efforts should be made to obtain as many outlets as possible. Some private traders, particularly if they are members, may be prepared to waive trade discount, but *never* take their goodwill for granted. Discount should always be offered, even if it is refused. Stocks should be regularly replenished.
— Turnover will increase if special point-of-sale containers can be offered free of charge to retailers. These need to attract attention but should be compact enough not to be a nuisance. With a little ingenuity they can easily be made out of strong cardboard.
— As the society's profit are greater on direct sales, copies should be available at *all* meetings and events.

Whether the trail is given away free or placed on sale, it is essential to launch it properly. Press notices must be sent to local papers, local radio and regional television with a copy of the trail and giving details of how it can be obtained. If possible, also arrange an inauguration by inviting a party of local dignitaries to be first to follow the trail—and notify the Press of this, too. As well as getting the trail off to a good start, lively publicity will be appreciated by distributors and advertisers. If display boards are provided to supplement the printed text, they should carry the information that they form part of a trail.

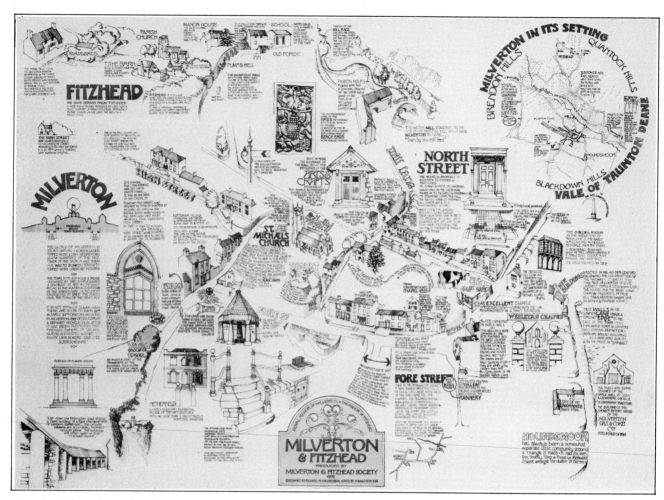

Attractive, informative and cautionary – a well-designed wallsheet produced by the Milverton and Fitzhead society in Somerset.

(16) Wallsheet

Application and technique In the home and in schools wallsheets are now probably more popular than ever before but so far they have been published only for a handful of towns outside the 'obvious' places such as Oxford, Cambridge, London and Stratford. Though by definition a wallsheet is difficult to use on the spot as a guide, it is an effective and flexible medium of interpretation. Possible forms are a mosaic or capriccio of buildings, or a stylised bird's-eye or isometric plan with key buildings and features drawn in.

To be worth printing—i.e. to ensure that people *want* to display it—a wallsheet needs to be well researched, well designed and well produced. It is best to begin by deciding what features of the area are to be highlighted. Then an overall lay-out can be devised for the sheet, and line-drawings executed, preferably by one and the same member to ensure consistency of conception. Design needs to be arresting enough to attract attention without being so elaborate as to swamp the subject-matter. Copy needs to be written by a member with knowledge, insight and the ability to write crisply and without too much jargon. Printing should be to a high standard on good-quality paper. The best results are often achieved by printing in one or two colours on a tinted paper. For advice on marketing, see section (15) (trails).

100

Example An excellent example of a wallsheet in the form of a bird's-eye view is 'Milverton and Fitzhead', produced in 1975 by the Milverton and Fitzhead Society in Somerset. As well as pinpointing and describing all the main landmarks, such as churches, chapels, schools and farms, this highlights other features which are less conspicuous, almost as important for the contributions they make to the townscape, but much more vulnerable—iron railings, Victorian polychromatic brickwork, and so on. 'Vacant' areas on the edge of the plan are used for the title and for essential background information about the town's setting and site. There is a cautionary element, too, as there should be: one particular corner is now too wide for the scale of the town and the text comments: 'The gap was required for sight lines for the car—one of the demands of the 20th century on a town which evolved when the horse was the fastest means of transport. It's a matter od discerning what is adaptation and what is destruction'.

Outlay and revenue Assuming that copy and artwork are produced free of charge, the cost of 1,000 wallsheets, printed letterpress to an A1 format, is likely to be about £250. If all 1,000 are sold (half by direct sales at a retail price of 50p and half at 33.3p—allowing for the usual trade discount of 33⅓%—to local retailers) a profit of £167 should accrue. This can be ploughed back for further interpretive or environmental work.

Promotion and marketing Much of the advice on trails (15) also applies to wallsheets.

(17) Guided Walks

The guided walk is one of the most effective interpretive media. It appears last of all in this manual not because it is unimportant but because if the guides are volunteers it involves little or no capital outlay. This is one of its advantages. Among the others are that participants can seek, and usually obtain, immediate answers to questions the guide's commentary may stimulate; and that if the party is a coherent one (e.g. in terms of age, interest of place of origin), the scope and/or level of treatment can be tailored to their needs.

In terms of participants, there are basically three types of guided walk:
(1) Those arranged in advance for a group resident in the area concerned
(2) Those arranged in advance for a group not resident in the area concerned
(3) Those arranged in advance but for all comers and not any particular group.

A guided walk (as here in Glasgow) is one of the best ways of sharing knowledge and understanding of an area – but the best guide/participant ratio is about 1:20

Many local amenity societies already organise walks of one or other kind. The second is probably the most popular because it affords an opportunity of introducing outsiders to features of charm and interest in the locality: if the guests are from another local amenity society it also offers scope for cross-fertilisation of ideas. The first seems less popular; perhaps it does not occur to many other local organisations that a walk round their own area might be interesting and enjoyable, and so they do not ask for the facilities. The third is the best way of catering for casual participants (mainly residents but in tourist towns also visitors) but so far only a handful of societies have tackled it. There are probably two reasons. First it requires a regular schedule of tours, and guides; and, second, it has to be advertised.

Charges are not normally made for walks of the first two kinds, though sometimes the guest organisation is discreetly advised that a donation to the host would not come amiss. Participants in 'open' tours are sometimes charged a small fee.

There is no doubt that local amenity societies in particular could do much to develop guided walks. Most, though they gladly provide them, tend to wait until they are *asked* by another organisation. It would be much better if they made their willingness more generally known. Every so often, for example, they could send a circular letter to other voluntary organisations in the locality and /or to local amenity societies and local history societies in the surrounding area indicating that, given reasonable notice, they can arrange a walk.

Subject to the availability of guides they could also launch short series of 'open ' tours. Publicity for these usually takes the form of small posters displayed in libraries, town halls, churches, tourist information centres, museums and hotels. These need not be expensive to produce and to begin with there is no reason why they should not be duplicated, perhaps with an electronic stencil used to provide a suitable illustration. The cost can be recovered by making a small charge for the tour. Alternatively a local authority may be willing to co-sponsor 'open' tours, at least to the extent of providing the necessary publicity material free of charge.

Though tours of this kind usually take place in the afternoon, organisations in towns which attract overnight visitors some-times arrange short evening tours. These are much appreci-ated by participants who often find themselves with spare time between arrival and an evening meal.

When walks are arranged in advance, a specimen copy of any relevant free leaflet should be sent to the person booking the service, and copies should be available for distribution to each member of the party on the day. The person booking the walk should also be asked what aspects will most interest the party and whether any other characteristics of the party need to be taken into account—whether for example most of the mem-bers are likely to be elderly.

Most guided walks provide and introduction to a particular locality, highlighting its main features of interest (usually including of course some that are not immediately apparent). Though these can play an important part in fostering under-standing and appreciation of a locality, there is also scope in most places for walks which concentrate on more specific themes–e.g. a conservation area, an industrial area, the legacy of a particular period or the work of a particular architect (cf. the lists given for Forchester on p. 37). Some of these topics may even be of sufficient interest for 'open' walks,

though in general these will not attract sufficient participants if the subject is too esoteric.

The length of guided walks is a key factor. However gifted the guide, a walk can become an ordeal if it lasts too long or involves too much footwork, and 90 minutes at a time is probably enough for most people. On the other hand, if visiting parties have come a long way, perhaps for the day, a single 90-minute walk may not be enough, and a longer walk may be provided, but with lunch or tea between the two laps. Preferably, too, to avoid any risk of monotony, there should be more than one guide, and the walk itself should be laced by visits *inside* particularly interesting buildings. These may include not only churches and museums but (in the case of pre-arranged walks) private houses (if the owners are willing) and factories, some of which welcome organised parties if arrangements are made well in advance. Contingency arrangements should be made in case wet weather sets in and if visiting parties come by coach they should be advised beforehand where to park and pick up.

Any organisation offering conducted tours needs to build up a team of trained guides. In all likelihood they will be volunteers, and there should be no lack of them, because by definition local amenity societies and similar organisations draw their support from people who are proud of their area, interested in it and (often but not always) knowledgeable about it. These are not the only requirements, however. The others are the right kind of personality and the ability to communicate information effectively.

In voluntary organisations it may be difficult to organise any formal training for guides—not because they lack the time, but because they are free at different times of day on different days of the week. In any case some may feel that formal instruction is unduly pretentious. In circumstances like these it may help to issue some duplicated 'Notes for Guides' like those printed opposite.

THE FORCHESTER SOCIETY

registered with the Civic Trust

Notes for Guides

We hope you will find these notes helpful. Much of the advice given is mere commonsense, but from experience we know that it helps to have a check-list of points to bear in mind.

Before you are asked to take your first guided walk arrangements will be made for you to join a group under one of our longer-serving guides.

Routes For visitors and outside groups the Society has devised two 90-minute walks - one in the town centre and one in the riverside area. Each can be extended by 30 minutes by the inclusion of optional detours. The town centre walk, as well as being available to parties who book in advance, is operated as an 'open' walk (open to all who turn up to join it) on Saturday and Sunday afternoons in the summer. The departure point is the Central Library forecourt in Miles Row. Full details of the routes, and the features of interest along them, are given in the 'Briefing Notes for Guides' you will be given with these notes.

Preparation It is a good idea to familiarise yourself with both walks by first reading the briefing notes and then following them with the notes in your hand. These are typed in double spacing so that you can record any queries, or additional points of interest. It should be possible to answer most queries by looking up one or other of the books on Forchester listed at the end, but in case of difficulty do not hesitate to ask the Guided Walks Organiser.

Welcoming a Group We try to ensure that no party consists of more than 20 people. If a visiting group is larger than this, we provide extra guides. When you meet your party for the first time, you should introduce yourself by name, and explain that the Society arranges these walks in order to foster fuller understanding and enjoyment of the town. You should go on to say how long the walk is expected to take, where it will finish and whether (e.g.) tea will be available at the end of it. At this stage you might enquire how many of the party know the town, and perhaps comment that you hope even those who know it will feel they know it better at the end of the walk. Finally before starting the walk you can give a very brief outline of the town's evolution (see Briefing Notes) and mention one or two of the interesting features the party will see. If wet weather threatens you can mention the contingency plans (see Briefing Notes). In case you are asked, you will need to know where there are public conveniences en route. To make sure that you do not lose any participants always count the party before you set off.

Technique Though elementary, the following points are worth restating. Speak clearly and not too quickly - at all events do not gabble! Gesticulate if you like (but not too much!) but do stand still. Look the party in the face - there is nothing more disconcerting than a guide who looks down at the ground as if it is about to erupt, up at the sky as if a flying saucer is about to land, or on one side or the other as if a building is about to fall down. After every chunk of explanation, allow a moment for questions. The question-and-answer process is one of the best ways of establishing a rapport with a party.

Your Briefing Notes provide answers to some of the most frequent questions; others you may be able to answer off your own bat; but if you simply don't know, say so, and if it seems practicable, offer to find the answer later.

On the Walk The Briefing Notes suggest convenient stopping places. These have been chosen not only because they provide good viewpoints but also as far as possible to save you raising your voice too much against the roar of traffic and to prevent the party causing too much of an obstruction to other pedestrians. Encourage the party to use pedestrian crossings wherever possible and warn them of any road hazards (one-way streets as well as blind corners). Ask them to keep together as far as possible and before you begin your commentary at a particular point make sure they have all arrived. Between stopping points try to chat to as many different members of the party as possible - and don't wait for them to take the lead. At all costs avoid being monopolised by one member.

Don't forget to adjust your commentary to allow for any special characteristics of the group. If some or all of them are from well outside the area, for example, you may have to explain some special local terms. Try to couch your explanations as gracefully as possible, e.g. don't say: 'Over Brown's the record shop, you can see some pargetting. This is ornamental plasterwork, and dates from about 1700'; but say instead: 'Can you all see Brown's the record shop? Good. You'll be able to see it has some ornamental plasterwork. The architects call this 'pargetting' and it dates from about 1700.'

You will find that your performance improves with experience. You will discard approaches or phrases which you notice fall flat, you will weave in those which you have tested and found effective. You may like to pass on any particularly useful tips to other guides.

<u>At the end of the Walk</u> Allow a last opportunity for questions and then give participants a brief idea of some of the other features of interest which it may not have been possible to include in the walk but which they may like to return to see one day on their own. Finally, remind them about any arrangements for meals (or let them know where these can be obtained), let them know about any shops that are particularly interesting, and (if relevant) advise them how to reach their coach.

<u>General</u> If you need any further advice or information, please get in touch with the Guided Walks Organiser.

Appendices

Dynamic change mirrored – literally – in a modern office block in Ipswich. Such scenes of sharp contrast are a rich quarry for urban interpretation. For better or for worse? People should be helped to make up their own minds.

Appendix 1

Check-List of Features of Interpretive Value

Before any interpretive work is planned, a stocktaking of the area's setting and fabric should be undertaken (cf pp 19–35). The aim should be to identify features of interpretive value, and it may be helpful to use a photocopy of the following check-list, tick those features which can be seen locally, and add any others which are not included. The list is in rough chronological order and not intended to be exhaustive.

Themes	Features	
Physical setting (including geology, physiography and climate)	Soil	Crops, stock, farming practice
	Fossils	Pasture, moorland, fells, heaths, commons
	Glacial deposits, erratics	Woodland, forestry
	Outcrops	Water-meadows, irrigation, glass-houses
	Earthquakes, earth tremors, faults, landslips	
	Waterfalls, swallow-holes, caves, caverns, potholes	Rainfall, snowfall, sunshine
	Gorges	Cloud types, fog, mist, haze
		Frost susceptibility
	Estuaries, rivers, creeks	Floods, droughts, storms, blizzards
	Tides, bores	
	Rivers, becks, burns, streams, springs	Windbreaks, walls, tree screens
	Fords	Windmills, windpumps
	Watersheds	Trees—habit
	River valleys, dry valleys	Watermills, reservoirs
	River terraces	Snow fences, snow ploughs
	Alluvial deposits, abandoned river courses, meanders	Skating, ski-ing
	Lakes, lochs, ponds, meres, peat deposits	Pumps, conduits, wells
	Marshes, bogs, fens	Building sites/aspects
		Roof pitch
	Hills, mountains, ridges	Snow boards
		Slate hanging, tarring of walls
	Natural harbours	
	Cliffs, headlands, spits	Street plan
	Saltings, beaches, dunes	People's attire (reflecting climate)
	Coastal erosion/accumulation	
	Landlocked 'islands' (e.g. Axholme, Oxney)	
	Quarries, chalkpits, clay pits, flint workings, gravel pits, brickworks	
	Opencast mines, deep mines	
	Railway/road/canal cuttings and embankments	
	Causeways	
	Building materials	
	Mineral-based industries	
	Track and road courses/deviations	
	Flora, exotics	
	Fauna, introductions	
	Seasonal migrations	
	Hibernation	
	Sea food	
	Freshwater fishing	
	Regional foods/dishes	

Themes	Features
Settlement patterns (cf Physical setting)	Landing place, natural harbour
	Estuary, river (access)
	River, stream, spring, aquifer (water supply)
	Soil, terrain
	Woodland (hunting, fuel, pig-keeping)
	Pasture
	Defensible/commanding site
	Secluded site
	Mineral resources (flint, metals, coal, salt)
	Fords, ferries, bridges
	Trackways, roads, railways
Prehistory, Roman occupation, Dark Ages	Place names (Celtic, Latin, Saxon, Scandinavian, French elements)
	Hill forts, causewayed camps
	Ditched settlements
	Flint mines
	Chamber tombs, cromlechs, barrows
	Stone circles/rows, monoliths
	Hill figures
	Trackways
	Preserved sites and monuments
	Holy wells, sacred springs/lakes/pools

Roman roads/settlements/bricks re-used
Sea walls (may now be well inland)
Field systems
Parish boundaries
Inscribed stones, early Christian crosses
Hundred meeting sites
Linear earthworks (Dykes)
Open field (strip) farming
Saxon church buildings/sites
Saxon cathedral foundations/diocesan boundaries
Saxon charters
Forest settlements/colonisation

Medieval
(Norman Conquest to Reformation)

Norman Conquest — Place names
Castles
Other Norman buildings (churches, abbeys etc)
New Towns
Town defences (walls, ditches)
New cathedrals/dioceses

The Church — Cathedrals, monasteries, collegiate churches, parish churches, chantries, chapels, shrines, hermits
Monastic property (land, livings, privileges)
Tithe barns
Hospitals (for sick, elderly, pilgrims)
Schools, universities
Music

Urban life — Manors, manor houses, manor courts
Markets, market places, market crosses
Decayed market towns
Fairs
Charters of incorporation, failed towns, rotten boroughs
Municipal records, insignia
Guildhalls, town halls, moot halls, sites
Church monuments, brasses
Trade guild buildings, sites, records
Bequests
Street plans, burgage plots
Planned towns
Street names
Churches, palaces, houses, shops, shambles
Bull rings, bear pits
Stocks, pillories, gallows, prisons (sites)
Conduits, leets, wells
Sun dials

Industry and Transport — Quays, wharves, sluices
Windmill sites/mounds
Watermill sites
Bridges
Roads, tracks, green lanes
Quarries, mines

Building — Evolution of styles
(Romanesque—Perpendicular)
Developing craftsmanship

Exploitation of regional resources (stone, flint, cob, timber etc)
Timber framing—introduction and development
Roofing technique and materials
Early brickwork

Rural life — Pattern of settlement
Moated houses and sites
Open fields/ridge and furrow
Water meadows
Hedges
Royal forests
Farmhouses and cottages

Wool industry — Wool churches, towns

Black Death — Deserted villages

Printing — Early books, printers, libraries

From Reformation

Reformation — Monastic ruins and sites, street names
Monastic churches as cathedrals/parish churches
Monastic buildings adapted for other uses
Mutilation of parish churches (rood-lofts, stained glass, murals etc)
Recusant families and their homes
Priest holes
Catholic/Protestant martyrdom sites/memorials

Immigrant minorities — Surnames, street names
Dutch/Huguenot/Jewish/West Indian/Indian/Pakistani etc quarters
Dutch/French/other immigrant churches
Synagogues (early)
Weavers' houses
Ethnic shops, clubs and cinemas

Market gardening — Abandoned and surviving sites in relation to markets served

Emigration — Points of embarkation
Place name 'doubles' abroad

Rise of Merchant Navy — Ports, quays, wharves, warehouses (and sites)
Custom Houses
Shipyards (and sites)
Docks
Lighthouses, lifeboat stations
Pilotage offices
Church monuments, statues
Foreign influence on architectural design

Rise of British Empire — Trading company buildings (and sites)
Naval dockyards
Barracks
Ordnance industry buildings (and sites)
Government buildings
Regimental museums
Church monuments, statues

Term	Description
Renaissance	Architecture, architectural detail Furniture
Elizabethan drama	Galleried inn yards, theatre sites Buildings associated with playwrights/plays Towns/streets used as settings
Municipal charity	Almshouses, doles, apprenticeship grants Endowed/charity schools Municipal improvements and amenities
Poor Laws and unemployment relief	Workhouses (and sites) Post World War I road construction Job Creation Programme schemes
Religious dissent (cf Immigrant minorities, Emigration)	Meeting houses, chapels, Salvation Army citadels Buildings/sites associated with Wesley, Spurgeon, Booth etc
Gothic survival	Building examples
Great Fires	Rebuilt areas Building materials (prohibition of thatch, timber framing etc) Widening of streets, provision of greens
Land reclamation	Drains, sea walls Windpumps, pumping engines Alluvial soil New roads
Plague	Plague pit sites
Religious observance—changes	Church furnishings (liturgical changes) Church restorations, re-introduction of stained glass High/Low Church character Suburban churches, tin churches, mission churches Vicarages/old vicarages Redundant churches Churches converted for other uses Church 'centres'
Rise of insurance industry	Fire-marks, fire-engine houses, manual engines Insurance offices Insurance agents' houses (brass plates)
Theatres	Building examples (and sites)
Smuggling	Caves, cliff paths 'Secret rooms/passages/entrances' Coastguard service buildings
Emergence of the developer	Early redevelopments on town mansion sites Terraces, squares, circuses Family estates
Rise of banking	Bank buildings and signs
Canals and navigations	Canals, navigations, warehouses Canal settlements, pubs, craft Connecting tramways (courses)
Brick and window taxes	Oversize bricks, mathematical tiles, weatherboarded construction Blocked windows
Pleasure gardens	Sites
Rise and decline of spas	Spa towns, buildings, wells, baths
Transportation	Points of embarkation Crimes (sites)
Turnpike roads and coaching	18th/19th century road improvements (embankments, cuttings, bridges, re-alignments) Tollhouses, bars, gates (and sites) Tollboards, milestones Coaching inns, stables Forges, wheelwrights' and coachbuilders' premises (and sites)
Industrial revolution	Associated buildings, mines, quarries and sites Derelict land Workers' housing, model villages
Enclosures	Landscape, field patterns
County hospitals and prisons	Building examples
Farm mechanisation etc	Horse gins, donkey wheels, treadmills Farm buildings Hedge removal/size of fields Cold stores Silos Disused barns/farmhouses Crop spraying (by tractor/from air) Intensive stock rearing units Widening of accesses for milk tankers etc
Steam power (cf Rise and decline of railways)	Stationary engines (and sites) Coal mines, connecting canals, tramways and railways Factory design Power stations
Gothic revival	Building examples (and sites) Furniture
Rise and decline of railways	Tramways (industrial) Inclined planes Railways (used/disused) Railway buildings (used/disused/converted) Railway ports Preserved railways
Rise of tourism	Seaside resorts Piers, jetties (steamer trips) Bathing machines, beach huts, lifeguards Railways Hotels, boarding-houses, week-end cottages Holiday camps, country cottages, holiday villages CTC/AA/RAC signs/facilities Charabancs, coaches and their liveries Long-distance coach services

Theme	Associated sites
	Coach parks, road houses Tea shops, restaurants, souvenir and antique shops Museums and interpretive facilities Information Centres Caravan parks, camping sites Long-distance walks
Cast iron in buildings	Associated buildings and foundries
Concrete in building	Associated buildings
Gas industry	Gasworks (and sites) Gas lighting (and vestiges) North Sea terminals
Parliamentary reform	Rotten boroughs Constituency boundaries Homes of enfranchised voters
Police	Police stations (disused/in use)
Penny post	Post offices, sorting offices Pillar boxes, letter boxes
Prefabricated building	Building examples old and new Factories
Local government reforms	Old/disused town halls/municipal offices/depots Monumental town halls Local offices/mini town halls
Mass production	Associated factories, transport facilities, workers' housing, outlets
Licensing laws	Inns, beerhouses, pubs, hotels (disused/in use) Coffee taverns, temperance hotels Breweries, hop gardens, oasts Distilleries Vineyards Bonded stores Theme pubs Children's rooms, beer gardens Off-licences
Decline of traditional customs	Survivals/revivals Associated sites
Music Hall	Associated buildings and sites Houses associated with performers
Outdoor advertising	Hoardings, neon signs Advertising drums
Building societies	Housing built for owner occupation Society HQs and offices
Cholera and water supply	Waterworks Reservoirs National water grid
Victorian self-help	Institutes, mechanics' institutions Co-operative society premises Cottage hospitals Allotments
Public health reform	Slum clearance Sewers and sewage works/outfalls Bye-law housing Municipal/private cemeteries, crematoria
Municipal waste disposal	Land reclamation (quarries, gravel workings, saltings) Incinerating plant Recycling facilities Associated transport facilities (coastal/rail/road)
Trade Unionism	Sites for mass meetings Buildings/sites associated with major disputes Union HQs, area offices, conference centres, convalescent homes Houses associated with major figures
National exhibitions/trade fairs	Sites and surviving buildings Architectural influence
Department stores	Buildings examples (converted/in use)
Chain stores	Building examples
Market halls	Building examples
Compulsory education	Board schools
Professional sport	Football/cricket grounds etc
Art Nouveau	Building examples Furniture and interior design Graphics
Municipal fire service	Fire stations, training schools Hydrants
Municipal housing	Building examples (houses, flats, high-rise blocks)
Preservationism	Restored buildings Over-restored buildings Facade retention Facsimiles Ancient Monuments Listed buildings Conservation areas Open air museums of buildings/buildings moved from original sites and re-erected
Garden City movement	Garden cities and villages Municipal housing estates of garden city type Speculative/spurious 'garden city' developments Green Belt
Electricity industry	Power stations (coal/oil fired, nuclear)—disused/in use Distribution network Coal mines, oil terminals
Telephone system	Exchanges (disused/in use) Distribution network (overhead/underground) Radio links

Rise and decline of tramways	Surviving systems Associated buildings and features Pattern of suburban development Abandoned inner suburban railway stations Museum tramways Manufacturers' premises
Cinema	Building examples (converted/in use) Studios (converted/in use)
Municipalisation	Municipal power stations (converted) Municipal tram/trolleybus/bus depots (in use/converted) Municipal water supply installations Street furniture relating to the above
Railway electrification	Examples (abandoned/in use) Equipment manufacturers' premises Pattern of suburban development
Internal combustion engine (general)	Manufacturers' premises (converted/in use) Service stations (converted/in use) Components industry premises Motor showrooms, used car lots Roads and lanes with surfaces dressed/laid for motor traffic (cf green lanes) Roadstone quarries, processing plant, transport (road/rail) Gravel extraction, processing, transport (road/rail) Oil industry premises/plant Housing lay-out, domestic garages (single/multiple) Traffic signs, traffic management schemes, guard rails, barriers Ribbon development Car parks (surface, multi-storey, underground) Road accident black spots, hospital accident centres and units Abandoned tramways/trolleybus systems/railways Declining rural bus services, post buses AA, RAC boxes, phones Noise, fumes, vibration, double glazing Vehicle scrapyards
Company amalgamations	Prestige HQs Derelict premises/plant Unemployment problems Growth of long-distance road haulage Corporate image, vehicle liveries Shopfront standardisation
World War I	War Memorials Defence installations (abandoned/in use) Premises rebuilt after bomb damage
Decline of domestic service	Basements, garrets, stabling adapted for new uses Infill housing in gardens of big houses Big houses split into flats Tradesman's entrances Domestic appliance manufacturing/retailing/servicing premises
Air transport	Aerodromes, airports, heliports, hovercraft terminals and access facilities (road/rail) Ancillary residential/commercial/hotel development Aircraft factories Airship/flying boat terminals (abandoned) and ancillary development Noise, double glazing
Road building for the motor vehicle (cf internal combustion engine (general))	Arterial roads, by-passes, ring and relief roads, motorways, dualling of major roads Road construction industry depots Road widening and other 'improvements' Blight/destruction/loss of agricultural land associated with the above
Modern movement in design	Building examples (including early buildings in the functional tradition) Furniture and interior design Graphics Street furniture
Rise of road haulage industry	Heavy goods vehicles Manufacturers' premises Road haulage depots/lorries parked on public highways at night and at week-ends Consolidation depots HGVs on international services (TIR vehicles) Overloading checks Abandoned rail goods facilities Road widening to ease corners for long vehicles, property destruction Physical damage to buildings, pavements, street furniture Noise, fumes, vibration, mud-spray on walls of roadside properties Blighted property/accommodation
Commuting	Pattern of development (including 'leaps' beyond Green Belts) Suburban railway depots Pattern of social life
Radio and television	Studios, monitoring service offices Manufacturers'/retailers' premises Transmitters (aerial installations) Domestic aerials, 'piped' systems Decline of cinema, music hall and theatre
Art Deco	Buildings examples Furniture and interior design Graphics
Motor sports	Motor racing circuits Associated noise and traffic congestion Road rally nuisance
World War II	War Memorials Defence installations (abandoned/in use) Areas/buildings rebuilt after bomb damage Bomb sites still derelict
Welfare State	New hospitals/hospital extensions Health centres Old people's housing

Nationalisation	Pre-nationalisation relics Industries HQs
Planning and associated legislation (cf Preservationism, Environmentalism)	Examples of successes and failures of development control Trees protected by TPOs National Parks, AONBs, SSSIs Subsidised transport services Homes improved with improvement grants, GIAs, Housing Action Areas (outside lavatories retained?) Village envelopes
High taxation of the rich	Stately homes and country houses open to the public National Trust properties Conversion of large houses into offices/flats/schools/conference centres etc Homes of tax exiles (Isle of Man and Channel Islands)
New and Expanding Towns	Examples Inner urban decay
Decline of small markets	Sites of disused markets
District and central heating	District heating installations Removal/absence of chimneys Double glazing Cleaner air
Comprehensive education	Building examples
University expansion	Building examples
System building	Building examples
Central area redevelopment	Examples Blight/destruction of useful resources
Containerisation	Sea/road/rail terminals
	Vehicles and vessels Decline of traditional docks Inland ports
Computerisation	Computer centres (buildings) Manufacturers' premises
Supermarkets, hypermarkets and 'shopping centres'	Examples Blight/loss of traditional shopping streets/corner shops Car parks Consolidation depots
Asset stripping	Derelict premises/plant/sites Unemployment problems
Regional development policies	Grant-aided factories and other facilities
Environmentalism	Sites of development/roads/airports averted by public concern Buildings/trees preserved/conserved Pedestrianisation, pedestrian priority streets Traffic restraint measures Bus priority schemes Width/weight restriction orders Bottle banks, other recycling facilities Section 8 Grants (new railway sidings) Conservation schemes aided by Government/local authority/charitable grant Local amenity society improvement/restoration schemes Re-opened canal facilities Interpretive facilities
Devolution and nationalism	National/regional HQs of Government offices National flags Bilingual signs
European Economic Community	Projects aided by EEC grants/loans (agriculture, commerce, tourism)

Appendix 2

Some Urban Heritage Interpretation Media: Capital and Running Costs £

Notes

(1) These examples are given for illustrative purposes only and actual costs will vary from area to area.

(2) The calculations are based on prices prevailing in Autumn 1978 and allowance should be made for the effects of inflation since this date.

(3) In most cases, a range of options is given, depending on the extent to which volunteers can undertake (for instance) design work. If a voluntary organisation such as a local amenity society can rely on its members to provide without charge at least some of the skills required, it can carry out interpretive work more cheaply than a local authority or other statutory body, which has to pay for all the expertise it needs.

(4) Medium 17 (Guided Walks) is omitted as no capital or maintenance costs are usually involved.

Capital Costs £

Medium	Building		Equipment		Displays		Printing		Total
	Purchase	Restoration & Conversion	Purchase	Materials only	Design & Execution	Execution only	Design & Printing	Printing only	
(A) DISPLAY MEDIA									
(1) Heritage Centre 3,000 sq ft of displays + 1,000 sq ft ancillary accommodation; costs of equipment *included* with costs of displays which also include £2,500 for purchase of bookshop stock									
(1a) Building given or at peppercorn rent; no restoration or conversion required; displays designed free of charge	—	—	—	—	—	12,500	—	—	12,500
(1b) As 1a, but fees charged for design of displays	—	—	—	—	32,500	—	—	—	32,500
(1c) As 1b, but purchase of suitable building at concessionary price required	20,000	—	—	—	32,500	—	—	—	52,500
(1d) As 1c, but restoration and conversion required	20,000	25,000	—	—	32,500	—	—	—	77,500
(1e) As 1d, but 50% of restoration/conversion costs met by grant(s)	20,000	12,500	—	—	32,500	—	—	—	65,000
(2) Display Cases with 'rotating' displays Set of 4 cases @ £1,250 each inclusive of installation in outdoor site									
(2a) Displays designed free of charge	—	—	5,000	—	—	500	—	—	5,500
(2b) Fees charged for design of displays	—	—	5,000	—	1,500	—	—	—	6,500

Medium	Building		Equipment		Displays		Printing		Total
	Purchase	Restoration & Conversion	Purchase	Materials only	Design & Execution	Execution only	Design & Printing	Printing only	
(3) Mini Heritage Centre									
300 sq ft; costs of equipment *included* with cost of displays									
(3a) Displays designed free of charge	—	—	—	—	—	2,000	—	—	2,000
(3b) Fees charged for design of displays	—	—	—	—	5,000	—	—	—	5,000
(3c) As 3b, but £1,000 allowed for purchase of sales stock (included with cost of displays)	—	—	—	—	6,000	—	—	—	6,000
(4) Audio-Visual									
(4a) 10/30 minute programme of up to 160 slides on single screen; 3 projectors; cassette recorder; tape-slide synchroniser; 3 heavy duty cassettes; booth constructed and programme produced free of charge (except for cost of materials)	—	—	1,250	200	—	—	—	—	1,450
(4b) As 4a, but charge made for building of booth	—	—	1,650	—	—	—	—	—	1,650
(4c) As 4b, but charge made for production of programme	—	—	1,600	—	500	—	—	—	2,100
(5) Display Case									
Single permanent display, inclusive of installation in outdoor site									
(5a) Display designed free of charge	—	—	1,250	—	—	125	—	—	1,375
(5b) Fees charged for design of display	—	—	1,250	—	375	—	—	—	1,625
(6) Vantage Point Key									
Masonry/brick pier with inset cast/engraved metal key									
(6a) Built and designed without charge	—	—	—	250	—	50	—	—	300
(6b) As 6a, but charge made for construction of pier	—	—	500	—	—	50	—	—	550
(6c) As 6b, but charge made for design of key	—	—	500	—	125	—	—	—	625
(7) Display Board									
Single outdoor board, inclusive of installation									
(7a) Board made and display designed free of charge	—	—	—	75	—	75	—	—	150
(7b) As 7a, but charge made for making of board	—	—	150	—	—	75	—	—	225
(7c) As 7b, but fees charged for design of display	—	—	150	—	200	—	—	—	350

Medium	Building		Equipment		Displays		Printing		Total
	Purchase	Restoration & Conversion	Purchase	Materials only	Design & Execution	Execution only	Design & Printing	Printing only	
(B) NON-DISPLAY MEDIA									
(8) Community Biography 1,000 copies printed offset-litho on coated paper with card cover									
(8a) 96pp A5 with 50 illustrations (20 artwork, 30 photographic); all artwork produced without charge	—	—	—	—	—	—	—	1,250	1,250
(8b) As 8a, but charge made for artwork (20 x £15)	—	—	—	—	—	—	1,550	—	1,550
(8c) As 8a, but 64pp A4	—	—	—	—	—	—	—	1,100	1,100
(8d) As 8c, but charge made for artwork (20 x £15)	—	—	—	—	—	—	1,400	—	1,400
(9) Listening Posts Set of 4 posts @ £208, with 4 battery packs @ £27, 1 charger @ £88, 1 access tool @ £18, 4 cartridges @ £8.75 (inclusive of tape) and 1 diagnostic unit @ £27: cost inclusive of installation at £25 per post	—	—	1,208	—	—	—	—	—	1,208
(10) Signed Trail									
(10a) 5,000 copies single A4 sheet folded in three, 6 illustrations, printed letterpress on coated paper; all artwork produced without charge; 16 cast aluminium plaques @ £25, all installed without charge (both sums included in printing cost)	—	—	—	—	—	—	—	700	700
(10b) As 10a, but charge made for artwork (6 x £10)	—	—	—	—	—	—	760	—	760
(10c) As 10b, but charge made for installation of plaques (16 x £15)	—	—	—	—	—	—	1,000	—	1,000
(11) Heritage Guide Cards (set)									
(11a) 1,000 copies each of 15 A5 cards, printed both sides offset litho in two colours; 2 illustrations per card (in all, 20 artwork, 10 photographic); all artwork produced without charge; 1,000 clear plastic A5 wallets	—	—	—	—	—	—	—	650	650
(11b) As 11a, but charge made for artwork (20 x £10)	—	—	—	—	—	—	850	—	850

Medium	Building		Equipment		Displays		Printing		Total
	Purchase	Restoration & Conversion	Purchase	Materials only	Design & Execution	Execution only	Design & Printing	Printing only	
(12) **Conservation Area Guide**—see 15c/15d									
(13) **Explorer's Kit**									
(13a) 1,000 copies 30 loose A4 sheets collated in printed manilla wallets, printed offset-litho on cartridge paper, 50 illustrations (20 artwork, 30 photographic); all artwork produced without charge	—	—	—	—	—	—	—	600	600
(13b) As 13a, but charge made for artwork (20 x £15)	—	—	—	—	—	—	900	—	900
(14) **Sound Trail** 10 players @ £30, 20 cassettes @ £1, 75 nickel cadmium batteries @ £3, 5 battery chargers @*	—	—	595	—	—	—	—	—	595
(15) **Trail**									
(15a) 5,000 copies single A4 sheet folded in three, 6 illustrations, printed letterpress on coated paper; all artwork produced without charge	—	—	—	—	—	—	—	300	300
(15b) As 15a, but charge made for artwork (6 x £10)	—	—	—	—	—	—	360	—	360
(15c) 5,000 copies A5 16pp booklet printed offset-litho on coated paper, card cover, 12 illustrations; all artwork produced without charge	—	—	—	—	—	—	—	625	625
(15d) As 15c, but charge made for artwork (12 x £15)	—	—	—	—	—	—	805	—	805
(16) **Wallsheet**									
(16a) 1,000 copies A1 sheet, printed letterpress on cartridge paper; artwork produced without charge	—	—	—	—	—	—	—	250	250
(16b) As 16a, but charge of £150 made for artwork	—	—	—	—	—	—	400	—	400

Annual Income and Expenditure £

Notes

(1) It is assumed in each case that all capital costs have been met and therefore that no loan charges have to be met.

(2) In the case of publications it is assumed that all stocks are sold in one year. If they are not (as will often be the case) allowance needs to be made for (a) the loss of interest on the capital represented by stocks; and (b) inflation. It is also assumed in each case that the direct/wholesale sales ratio is 50/50.

(3) The general notes at the beginning of this Appendix should also be consulted.

Medium	Expenditure								Income			NET RETURN (+) or COST (−)
	Rates and Advertising	Insurance	Heating & Lighting	Maintenance	Depreciation (Equipment & Displays)	Design & Printing	Printing	TOTAL EXPENDITURE	Admissions/ Hire Fees	Sales	TOTAL INCOME	
(A) DISPLAY MEDIA												
(1) Heritage Centre 4,000 sq ft gross; voluntarily staffed and managed; bookshop with stock value at £2,500 wholesale—sales figures represent *net margin* on sales; annual admissions 10,000 @ 30p/7,500 @ 40p/6,000 @ 50p												
(1a) £200 spend on advertising, 100% rate remission	200	500	900	500	1,000	—	—	3,100	3,000	1,000	4,000	+ 900
(1b) As 1a, but only 50% remission of £1,000 rates	700	500	900	500	1,000	—	—	3,600	3,000	1,000	4,000	+ 400
(1c) As 1b, but Centre closed from October to March inclusive—admissions and sales 25% less, heating and lighting 67% less	700	500	300	500	1,000	—	—	3,000	2,250	750	3,000	± 0
(2) Display Cases with 'rotating' displays 4 cases @ £1,250 each; no rent or rates charged; outdoor sites	—	100	—	120	500	—	—	720	—	—	—	− 720

Medium	Expenditure								Income			NET RETURN (+) or COST (−)
	Rates and Advertising	Insurance	Heating & Lighting	Maintenance	Depreciation (Equipment & Displays)	Design & Printing	Printing	TOTAL EXPENDITURE	Admissions/ Hire Fees	Sales	TOTAL INCOME	
(3) Mini Heritage Centre 300 sq ft gross; sited in building in busy location; no rent or rates charged												
(3a) No sales point provided	—	50	—	—	500	—	—	550	—	—	—	− 550
(3b) Sales point provided; stock valued at £1,000 wholesale; manned voluntarily half daily throughout year; sales figures refer to *net margin* on sales	—	50	—	—	500	—	—	550	—	300	300	− 250
(4) Audio-Visual 10/30 minute programme of up to 160 slides on single screen; 3 projectors; cassette recorder; tape-slide synchroniser; 3 heavy duty cassettes; indoor site; no rent or rates charged	—	25	—	75	150	—	—	225	—	—	—	− 225
(5) Display Case 1 case @ £1,250; no rent or rates charged; outdoor site	—	15	—	30	125	—	—	170	—	—	—	− 170
(6) Vantage Point Key Masonry pier with inset cast/engraved metal key; outdoor site, no rent or rates charged	—	10	—	5	60	—	—	75	—	—	—	− 75
(7) Display Board Single outdoor board; no rent or rates charged	—	10	—	20	20	—	—	50	—	—	—	− 50

Medium	Expenditure								Income			NET RETURN (+) or COST (−)
	Rates and Advertising	Insurance	Heating & Lighting	Maintenance	Depreciation (Equipment & Displays)	Design & Printing	Printing	TOTAL EXPENDITURE	Admissions/ Hire Fees	Sales	TOTAL INCOME	
(B) NON-DISPLAY MEDIA												
(8) Community Biography												
(8a) 1,000 copies 96pp A5; 50 illustrations (20 artwork, 30 photographic); all artwork produced without charge; price retail £2.25, wholesale £1.50	—	—	—	—	—	—	1,250	1,250	—	1,875	1,875	+ 625
(8b) As 8a, but charge made for artwork	—	—	—	—	—	1,550	—	1,550	—	1,875	1,875	+ 325
(8c) As 8a, but 64pp A4; price retail £1.95, wholesale £1.30	—	—	—	—	—	—	1,100	1,100	—	1,625	1,625	+ 525
(8d) As 8c, but charge made for artwork	—	—	—	—	—	1,400	—	1,400	—	1,625	1,625	+ 225
(9) Listening Posts set of 4 as specified in Capital Cost table; insurance and maintenance @ 10% of capital value, depreciation at 20% (batteries 50%); 5,000 hirings of listening tubes per annum @ 25p; purchase of 1,000 listening tubes @ £130 and 4,000 replacement earpieces @ £10.75 per 1,000 included in maintenance costs	100	120	—	293	274	—	—		1,250	—	1,250	+ 463
(10) Signed Trail												
(10a) 5,000 copies single sheet A4 folded in three, 6 illustrations, printed letterpress on coated paper; all artwork produced without charge; price retail 10p, wholesale 6.7p	—	—	—	—	20	—	300	320	—	416	416	+ 96
(10b) As 10a, but charge made for artwork (6 x £10)	—	—	—	—	20	360	—	380	—	416	416	+ 36

Medium	Expenditure								Income			NET RETURN (+) or COST (−)
	Rates and Advertising	Insurance	Heating & Lighting	Maintenance	Depreciation (Equipment & Displays)	Design & Printing	Printing	TOTAL EXPENDITURE	Admissions/ Hire Fees	Sales	TOTAL INCOME	
(11) Heritage Guide Cards												
(11a) 1,000 copies each of 15 A5 cards, printed both sides offset-litho in two colours; 2 illustrations per card (in all, 20 artwork, 10 photographic); artwork produced without charge; 1,000 clear plastic wallets A5; price retail per set £1.20, wholesale 80p	—	—	—	—	—	—	650	650	—	1,000	1,000	+ 350
(11b) As 11a, but charge made for artwork (20 x £10)	—	—	—	—	—	850	—	850	—	1,000	1,000	+ 150
(12) Conservation Area Guide—see 15c/15d												
(13) Explorer's Kit												
(13a) 1,000 copies 30 loose A4 sheets, collated in printed manilla wallets, printed offset-litho on cartridge paper, 50 illustrations (20 artwork, 30 photographic); all artwork produced without charge; price retail £1.20, wholesale 80p	—	—	—	—	—	—	600	600	—	1,000	1,000	+ 400
(13b) As 13a, but charge made for artwork (20 x £15)	—	—	—	—	—	900	—	900	—	1,000	1,000	+ 100
(14) Sound Trail 10 players @ £30, 20 cassettes @ £1, 75 nickel-cadmium batteries @ £3, 5 battery chargers @ £10; hire charge 40p; 5 hirings a day October/March; 15 a day April/September; trail available 5 days a week; to allow commission to hire point 20% *already deducted* from hire fees	200	50	—	100	75	—	—	425	768	—	768	+ 343

Medium	Expenditure								Income			NET RETURN (+) or COST (−)
	Rates and Advertising	Insurance	Heating & Lighting	Maintenance	Depreciation (Equipment & Displays)	Design & Printing	Printing	TOTAL EXPENDITURE	Admissions/ Hire Fees	Sales	TOTAL INCOME	
(15) Trail												
(15a) 5,000 copies single A4 sheet folded in three, 6 illustrations, printed letterpress on coated paper; all artwork produced without charge; price retail 10p, wholesale 6.7p	—	—	—	—	—	—	300	300	—	416	416	+ 116
(15b) As 15a, but charge made for artwork (6 x £10)	—	—	—	—	—	360	—	360	—	416	416	+ 56
(15c) 5,000 copies A5 16pp booklet printed offset-litho on coated paper, card cover, 12 illustrations; all artwork produced without charge; price retail 25p, wholesale 16.7p	—	—	—	—	—	—	625	625	—	1,041	1,041	+ 416
(15d) As 15c, but charge made for artwork (12 x £15)	—	—	—	—	—	580	—	805	—	1,041	1,041	+ 236
(16) Wallsheet												
(16a) 1,000 copies A1 sheet, printed letterpress on cartridge paper; artwork produced without charge; price retail 50p, wholesale 33.3p	—	—	—	—	—	—	250	250	—	417	417	+ 167
(16b) As 16a, but £150 charge made for artwork	—	—	—	—	—	400	—	400	—	417	417	+ 17

Appendix 3

Fund-Raising for Local Amenity Societies and Similar Organisations

Note
Advice on *grants* from public and private bodies is given on pp. 42-46

All costs quoted are as obtaining in Autumn 1978 and inclusive of VAT at 8%—where applicable—but exclusive of carriage—usually payable by the purchaser. Except in the unlikely event that their trading turnover exceeds £10,000 per annum, societies need not make VAT returns: this means that VAT cannot be recovered, and allowance has been made for this in calculating gross profit margins. Addresses of suppliers are given the first time they are mentioned.

More and more national conservation organisations, like the Royal Society for the Protection of Birds, the National Trust and the Association of Nature Conservation Trusts, derive a proportion of their income from trading activities. Many of the 'lines' serve directly or indirectly to promote the organisation's particular interests, so there is a publicity pay-off as well as a financial return. The same principles can be applied by local societies, though on a more modest scale. A picture postcard or slide view of an important local building or street can not only make a small profit, but will help to stimulate interest in the area and its conservation. A ball-point pen or pencil die-stamped with the society's name will help to publicise its work as well as raise money. Not a lot of capital is needed to make a start—less than £8 for a gross of ball-point pens, less than £20 for 500 picture postcards.

A word of warning, however, at the outset. A society which starts a trading operation, however small, must be prepared to do a bit of marketing, too. Otherwise turnover may be so slow that, taking inflation into account, the operation results in a loss rather than a profit. So a society launching a product must mention it repeatedly in its newsletter, make sure it is always on sale at meetings, and (if it is an exclusive line such as a picture postcard) send a press notice to the local Press and radio.

There are basically three kinds of merchandise that can make money for a society: the *exclusive product*, such as a picture postcard published by the society; the *'personalised'* product, such as a die-stamped pencil; and the ordinary *non-exclusive, non-personalised product* obtained from a wholesaler who supplies voluntary organisations. The third and last kind is perhaps the least promising. Apart from the fact that ordinary merchandise cannot also serve as a vehicle for publicising the society, trading in it may be seen by local shopkeepers as an infringement of their own territory. Though the infringement may seem insignificant, it is easy to see that if *every* voluntary organisation started general trading activities shopkeepers would definitely suffer. In other words what a society gained in income from this source it might lose in local goodwill.

Exclusive Products

Because of its specialised knowledge a local amenity society is well-placed to market exclusive products which reflect the character and development of its area. These may include picture postcards, colour slides, facsimiles of old prints and maps, histories, guides, trails and pamphlets. Unless the society is one of the very few with its own permanent shop window, and probably even if it is, it should try to come to some arrangement whereby its lines are on sale in appropriate local shops. Sometimes members who have shops will agree to stock the lines without receiving any discount, but even if a discount has to be allowed for, it is usually worthwhile because wider distribution will increase turnover.

Picture postcards These can provide good openings, if only because in most places the commercial range has dwindled to a few hackneyed views. The cards can be reproduced from photographs, slides or line drawings. If reproduced from colour photographs or slides, special blocks have to be made and the minimum economic run is 2,500 though some printers require a minimum order of 5,000. If reproduced from black-and-white originals, the cards can either be produced by one of the specialist firms or be printed offset-litho using a half-tone screen. Line drawings can be reproduced offset-litho or letterpress. Commercial postcard publishers employ their own photographers, but local societies will probably be able to rely on their own members to produce suitable photographs or drawings (advice on environmental photography is given in

Appendix 4, pp 128-132). There is often a ready market for views reproduced from old photographs, in which case help will be needed from a member with the equipment to make copy negatives. It needs to be borne in mind here that the copyright of a photograph is vested in the photographer until 50 years after his death. The best subjects are those which incorporate plenty of street life of the period. Their popular appeal, though not necessarily their technical quality, is sometimes enhanced by 'vignetting' them and reproducing them in sepia (rather than black) or on toned paper (rather than white). It is important for all photographs to be of high technical and artistic quality—a 'flat' or unimaginatively-composed view taken on an overcast day is unlikely to sell well, however attractive the subject. Equally, drawings need to be clear, fluent and unfussy. Three firms with experience of supplying photographic cards to local societies are English Life Publications Ltd (Lodge Lane, Derby, DE1 3HE), Pamlin Prints (73 Temple Road, Croydon, Surrey CR0 1HW) and Cotswold Collotype Ltd (Britannia Mill, Wootton under Edge, Gloucs.) For £25.92 *English Life* can supply 500 black-and-white cards of the standard size (3½"×5½"), with the captions on the front. If these are sold at 8p each, the gross profit amounts to £14.08. Because of the larger quantities involved, the minimum outlay for colour cards is much higher and probably beyond the reach of most societies. However profit margins are higher. 5,000 standard-size cards cost £145.00 and at a minimum selling price of 8p gross profits are £255.00. *Pamlin Prints*, who specialise in black-and-white, require a smaller minimum order—of 250. The cost is £18.00 and when the cards are sold at 8p each there is a gross return of £2.00. Pamlin are particularly keen to collaborate with local societies in the preparation of postcard-packs, consisting of five views, some of which may be 'period' ones. They also have a very wide range of 'period' cards from many parts of the country which societies can buy in relatively small quantities and re-sell at a useful profit. Cotswold Collotype can produce 500 cards for £17.90, and at a selling price of 8p these will yield a gross profit of £22.10.

Colour cards can be obtained from such firms as *English Life* and *Beric Tempest* (Temprint Works, St Ives, Cornwall). English Life require a minimum order of 5,000 and charge about 3.5p a card. Beric Tempest will accept orders for 2,500 at 3.4p each, and for 5,000 at 2p each. Thus though the minimum initial outlay is higher for colour than for black-and-white, the net profit can be higher.

The suggested retail price of 8p per card is higher than that of most commercial cards, which sell for 5p or even less.

However, societies with experience in the field find that customers will willingly pay the extra penny or two for an exclusive card otherwise unobtainable.

Christmas Cards The number of societies which publish Christmas Cards increases every year and this type of publication can offer a quick return in terms both of profit and public interest. Such cards usually feature a drawing by a member of some interesting local building or scene—perhaps even one that is under threat. When publishing for the first time it is best not to order too many (perhaps about 2,000), but once the tradition has been established the market will increase and orders of 5,000 or more can safely be placed. The card needs to be launched at the end of September or beginning of October and sales are improved (not impaired) if an illustration can be published as part of a news item in the local Press. A society selling 5,000 cards at only 8p each may expect to make a gross profit of £100 or more.

Colour slides Like that of picture postcards, the commercial range of colour slides is often restricted to one or two prominent buildings. Here again a society can take advantage of the opportunity to highlight other interesting buildings or views. All that is needed to begin with is the help of a member who is a capable photographer and less than £25 in capital. For £21.25 *English Life* will supply 250 copies of a single slide. With a suggested retail price of 15p, these should yield £16.25 gross profit. Sets of slides may sell more readily, but a bigger initial investment is needed—£75.00 for 250 sets of three, yielding a gross profit of £37.50. An unusual novelty is a 'key view'—a key chain with a 35 mm colour slide enclosed in a transparent fob. For the minimum order of 250 the charge is £47.50 and the gross profit (at a 30p selling price) is £27.50.

Ties These are perhaps better seen as a means of publicising a society or its area than as a way of raising funds, though they can fulfil both objectives. Modern techniques mean that ties can be woven to incorporate a wide range of motifs—emblems, flowers and buildings, for example—either singly or in multiple. One manufacturer is *Tudor Ties Ltd* (42 Wellingborough Road, Rushden, Northants NN10 9YN), who can supply 150 ties incorporating a 2-colour design for £220.50. If these are re-sold at £2.00 each a gross profit of £79.50 will accrue. Smaller quantities (down to 50) can be ordered, but the unit cost is then more than 50% higher, and the ties can be seen less as a fund-raiser than as a means of expressing members' allegiance to the society.

Facsimiles of old prints and maps Depending on the size of the original, these can be produced either as postcards or Christmas Cards or in a size suitable for framing. Experience suggests that the smaller format sells more readily. Reproduced offset-litho they can be sold quite cheaply but still yield a useful profit.

Books and pamphlets Societies have published hardback books but the investment required is well beyond the reach of the average society. Paper-back booklets are a more realistic proposition, particularly if printed offset-litho or run off on a duplicator. Costs may be reduced by the inclusion of local advertising, which can also add interest.

The subject-matter that probably offers the most scope is the historical, and it is a good idea to publish a numbered series of monographs. Purchasers will then tend to buy each new title as it comes out, often regardless of whether at first sight the specific topic interests them. It is helpful to include a foreword (by some local worthy) a contents list and biographical notes about the author. An index should also be featured if possible. It is a legal requirement that copies should be lodged free of charge in certain 'copyright libraries' (see p. 89) but this is no handicap, for deposit in the British Library will ensure (ultimately) an entry in the British National Bibliography, which will help to boost sales outside the area. It is also a good idea to send full details to J Whitaker & Sons Ltd (12 Dyott Street, London WC1A 1DF) for inclusion in *The Bookseller* and of course to send review copies to appropriate papers and journals.

One of the simplest ways of producing booklets is on a duplicator. Though the appearance and 'feel' will be inferior to that of printed work, good results are possible if sufficient care is taken with design and production. With the aid of electronic stencils illustrations can be included, though the standard of reproduction (particularly with photographs) is poorer than by other means. The initial outlay need be quite small, for the minimum economic run is about 100 copies. Particularly if a society owns its own duplicator (and many do), and can turn to its own voluntary typists, profit margins can be handsome. For instance in these circumstances a 24-page A4 booklet, with an illustrated card cover, costs about £9 for 100 copies. If these are sold at 25p each (and they will probably sell like the proverbial hot cakes), they will yield a gross profit of £16, or 16p a copy.

Margins will of course be reduced if the society does not possess, or have access to, a duplicator or if it has to pay for the stencils to be cut. Societies, except the smallest, which do not already possess a duplicator probably ought to consider buying one, for they can be so useful for such a variety of purposes—the production of agendas, minutes, press notices programmes and so on, besides booklets. New prices (allowing for 10% discount to charities) range from about £200 for hand-operated machines to £500 for electrics. Good second-hand machines are often available quite cheaply and many societies start with one of these and then 'trade-up' to a new machine. For booklets the only other requirement is a heavy-duty stapler which (if it cannot be borrowed) will cost about £25 (or about £45 in the case of an electric).

Personalised Products

Though the range of personalised products is wide, their local appeal is less than that of exclusive lines, and the society marketing them will be in closer competition with other good causes. However the initial investment is often very low, and the merchandise certainly helps to keep the society's name to the fore.

Ballpoint pens Silk-screened or die-stamped with an organisation's name, these are perhaps the most popular personalised product, and are available from a number of suppliers. *Harris Pencils Ltd* (P.O. Box 125, Lyon Way, Hatfield Road, St Albans, Herts AL4 0LD) offer 144 non-refillable ballpoints for £8.19, which can be sold at 10p each to make a gross profit of £6.21. Alternatively 150 of a better quality retractable ballpoint can be bought for £25.50, enabling a society to make a gross profit of £12.00 if the pens are sold for 25p each. A good range is also available from *Westfield Fund Raising Aids* (Westfield House, Helena Street, Birmingham B1 2RJ), who claim to be the United Kingdom's biggest supplier. The retail price of their lowest-price ballpoint could be an attractive 10p, but a society which spends £10.50 on a minimum purchase of 200 will still make £9.50 gross profit. Top of the range is the stylish 'Trio', a robust retractable. £5.55 gross profit can be made from a quantity of 100, which cost £9.45, if the selling price is 15p. *English LIfe* can incorporate line-drawings (of buildings, for example), as well as lettering. There is a range of three pens, all refillable and retractable. 500 of the 'Popular' cost £35.00 and when sold at 12p each yield a gross profit of £25.00. The 'Streamline' is a more robust pen, involving the same outlay and yielding the same profit, but requiring a minimum purchase of only 250 (selling price is 27p). Top of the range is the 'Golden Satin', with a metal body. £63.75 is needed for the minimum quantity of 250 and when sold at 42p each these yield a gross profit of £41.25.

Badges Laminated badges are particularly popular with children, who often collect them. Printed with lettering and design, they are also a good publicity media. *Westfield Fund Raising Aids* and *English Life* can both supply 1,000 1¼" badges for £45.00, yielding gross profits of £11.00 if the selling price is 6p each. Westfield can also supply smaller quantities of badges: 200 cost £12.00 if only lettering is used.

Others

A wide range of other personalised merchandise is available. An *English Life* speciality is packs of fudge or assorted toffees in wrappers bearing the name of the sponsor and an illustration of a building. The outlay for the minimum order of 80 200-gram packs is £27.60 and as these retail at 50p each the gross profit is £12.40. Book matches with well-designed and colourful covers can have special material (text and illustrations) printed on the inside cover by *Venture Matches* (Best Street, Kirkham, Preston, Lancashire PR4 2JD). 500 books 8″ long cost £75.60, yielding a gross profit of £49.40 if sold at 25p each. Longer 13″ books are also available. Books can also be personalised throughout—i.e. can have special pictorial material and text on the front and back covers respectively. The minimum order is then 5,000. The price for 5,000 books 4″ long is £324.00, and these will yield a gross profit of £176.00 if sold at 10p each. Blackpool Civic Trust had some very attractive match books produced by Venture Matches to help raise funds for their scheme to restore a 'Dreadnought' tram.

Non-exclusive, Non-'Personalised' Products

Products which are neither exclusive nor personalised will appeal less to local loyalties but may still be a useful means of raising funds. Care again needs to be taken not to infringe the livelihood of local traders, and large-scale investment should not be undertaken without prior test-marketing.

One firm (among several) which specialises in selling general merchandise to clubs and societies is CWAD (Manchester) Ltd (39 Great Ducie Street, Manchester 3), who require a minimum order of £20-worth of goods. Their range includes clothing, textiles, watches and jewellery. As illustrations, dozen-prices for men's cotton handkerchiefs are £1.35, for neck-purses £3.50 and for zodiac pendants £2.50. Mark-ups are left to purchasers, and catalogues are available on request.

Venture Matches can supply their attractive book matches in unpersonalised form. The minimum order is £50, and display units are supplied free of charge. 250 books 13″ long cost £64.80, yielding a gross profit of £40.20 if sold at 50p each.

Local Interest Books One kind of product that is neither exclusive nor personalised but will appeal to most members and friends is the book or booklet of local interest. The opportunities for societies to issue their own publications have already been described, but it may also be worthwhile buying small stocks of relevant titles from other publishers. However, turnover is likely to be too slow to make the operation worthwhile unless vigorous marketing tactics are adopted.

Titles should be hand-picked by a member with insight into what topics are likely to be of interest. Sales will probably be highest if the titles are not available off-the-shelf at the nearest bookseller's. Examples are Shire Publications' series of 'Discovering' paperbacks and the Oakwood Press railway histories (also in paperback). Interesting titles may also be available from such non-commercial sources as county and district councils, universities and other societies in the area. Discounts from commercial publishers are normally 33⅓%, though they may be scaled down for very small orders. Other publishers usually offer smaller discounts of around 15%. It is important to note that under the Net Book Agreement it is forbidden to sell books (except remainders) at 'cut prices'. Anyone infringing this Agreement will have their sources of supply cut off.

Development Areas (Spring 1979): grant may be available within these for tourist facilities and amenities (see p 44).

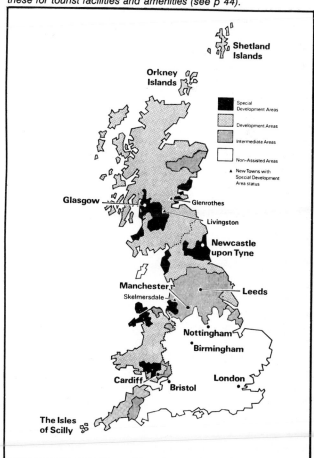

Appendix 4

Environmental Photography for local amenity societies and similar organisations

Equipment

Published statistics on leisure are rather coy about photography, but it is a fair bet that there are more camera-owning than car-owning households, and that 2-camera families far outnumber 2-car ones. Some enthusiastic amateurs own equipment whose value runs well into four figures, others make do with nothing more ambitious than a vintage box camera or a simple 'Instamatic'. What kind of equipment is best for environmental photography?

There is no simple answer, except perhaps that for most purposes expensive equipment is not essential. The simplest camera on sale today, or for that matter an old box camera which is still in working order, can produce good photographs if its limitations are accepted. It does have to be held still (like any other camera), it will not take pictures by twilight, it needs to be at least 5′ away from the subject, and if enlargements over 'enprint' size are made, they may lack definition.

But, granted that a wide range of cameras is available, how can they be deployed to the best advantage? It is best to consider each type in turn.

Rollfilm cameras, using 120 or 127 film, are less popular than they used to be, partly because they tend to be bulky, partly because they take longer to load and usually need loading more often than other types. Nowadays they are available mostly in the form of twin-lens reflex cameras (TLRs), but until the advent of the 126 cartridge (*see below*) rollfilm was the mainstay of the snap-shot market. Before 35mm film became popular, it was also used in folding (bellows) cameras, many of which remain in use.

Most TLRs cost £90 or more, though one simplified model (the Lubitel) sells at less than £15. All have the advantages of good lenses, a range of speeds, a large negative (6cm×6cm) from which big enlargements are possible, and a generous viewfinder which presents an image the same size as the negative. Focussing is done with the viewfinder and mistakes are therefore unlikely. An exposure meter will be needed if one is not built in.

Older folding cameras are by no means to be despised, though they are a little slower to use. Many of them feature excellent shutters and lenses, some of them rangefinders.

Some produce really large negatives 6cm×9cm (8 on 120 film) while others, taking 16 frames on the smaller 127 film, produce small negatives 3cm×4cm and are not much bigger than a modern pocket camera. Even the simpler folding cameras, such as a Vest Pocket Kodak of 1915 vintage, can yield good results in the right hands.

35mm cameras, the most popular with keen amateurs, use edge-perforated film 35mm wide of the kind originally devised, and still used, for commercial film-making. Negative size is quite small—normally 24×36mm, though 'half-frame' cameras yield a smaller 18×24mm. Taking 20 or 36 exposure cassettes, the cameras are easier to load, and need loading less often, than roll-film types. Half-frame models need new films even less frequently, as 40 or 72 shots are possible on the standard film. However this may mean film is wasted if, say, only a dozen photographs are needed urgently. The original 35mm cameras were all viewfinder types, but most photographers now prefer the single-lens reflex (SLR) in which composition and focussing are both done through the actual camera lens. Though in general SLRs are dearer and bulkier than other 35mm cameras, all have the key advantage that interchangeable lenses can be fitted quickly for different purposes—a telephoto for long-distance work, for example. Some ordinary 35mm cameras have this feature, but the best are very expensive. However the *'compact'* 35mm camera, without through-the-lens viewing or interchangeable lenses, remains popular because it is lighter and easier to handle than an SLR. Two inexpensive 35mm cameras, both costing less than £15, are the Cosmic Symbol and the Boots Beirette. Though simply built and without automatic exposure control, they feature good lenses capable of high-quality results.

Many 35mm cameras feature automatic exposure systems, freeing the user from the need to carry an exposure meter and in some cases from setting lens apertures and shutter speeds. These are convenient but for many townscape photographs the manual over-ride available in more expensive cameras is useful to cope with varying subject light intensities.

126, 'Rapid' and 110 cameras, using a plastic cartridge containing enough film for 12 or 20 exposures, are even easier to load than 35mm types. Yielding small negatives 28×28mm, the 126 format was introduced mainly for the snapshot market, and most cameras are simple ones with few controls and not much versatility. *Rapid cameras* are similar but use ordinary 35mm film in special cassettes and take slightly smaller negatives 24×24mm. They are no longer manufactured and even the 126 format is gradually being superseded by the tiny *110 film,* used in pocket cameras to produce diminutive negatives 13×17mm. Though this format is suitable for enlargments up to en-print size, only the more expensive 110 cameras have lenses capable of producing negatives fit for enlargement to half- or full-plate size. A good compact 35mm camera (£40 to £60) costs no more and is a bettter investment, unless there is a need for a camera that can always be carried in pocket or handbag.

Several 35mm cameras (mostly rather expensive ones), as well as some quite cheap 126 and 110 cartridge cameras feature a special type of electronic exposure control enabling pictures to be taken automatically and without flash in subdued light—for example indoors or in well lit streets at night. This is a useful facility, as flash is not usually powerful enough to throw more than 30ft or so and, unless 'bounced', is liable to cause distracting reflections. As time-exposures of up to 30 seconds, or even longer, may be involved, a tripod is essential and subjects with moving figures or vehicles must be avoided.

Which is best? Which of all these are best for environmental photography? It depends on the purpose to which the photographs are to be put. For survey work in normal lighting conditions the automatic compact 35mm camera, or a 126 type with an electronic shutter, have most to recommend them. In some cases a better-quality automatic 110 may be sufficient. The same equipment will be adequate for 'working' photographs needed to accompany representations to the authorities.

However most 110 or 126 cameras are unlikely to be capable of delivering the top-quality negatives needed for enlargement for exhibitions, publications, press notices and public inquiries or for reproduction as picture postcards. Here a good-quality 35mm camera (whether SLR or compact) is needed, or better still, perhaps, because of its larger negative size, a TLR or other well-equipped rollfilm camera.

Special Equipment For special purposes special equipment will be needed. Shots of inaccessible buildings or details will be impossible without a telephoto lens. Flash will be needed in some circumstances, for example to photograph details of the construction of a medieval roof where there is little or no daylight. In some 35mm and 110 cameras the lens aperture is automatically adjusted by the focussing mechanism and this saves complicated calculations. Old photographs can be copied with an SLR, using extension tubes if need be to bring the lens close enough to the subject, or with other cameras using supplementary close-up lenses. Even quite simple cameras can be used for this purpose, though an SLR yields the best results. Some societies buy Polaroid cameras so that in the event of emergency (the unauthorised felling of a protected tree, for example) a photograph is instantly available. For other equipment, it goes without saying, it is best to rely on members who already possess it and who are willing to take photographs for the society.

Films used for snapshot photography are normally 'medium-speed' ones (between 50 and 125 ASA) which respond well in normal daylight. 'Slower' films (below 50 ASA) which need longer exposure are less 'grainy' when enlarged and are well worth using if enlargements over full-plate size are needed. 'Faster' films (over 125 ASA up to 500 ASA, though some may be 'pushed' further) are useful when light is likely to be poor. Though grainier than other films, they produce excellent results in a quality camera and some professionals use them all the time. Films are expensive, particularly when used in quantity for a pictorial survey or similar purpose, and some keen amateurs save money by buying bulk lengths of 100' and using a special loader to fill their own 35mm cassettes. Otherwise it may be worth experimenting with the 'outdated' films often available at half-price or less. Almost always these prove perfectly satisfactory. It is also possible to save money by buying films in packs of 5 or more, for example from some of the dealers who advertise in *Amateur Photographer* and similar magazines, or by taking advantage of one of the 'free film' developing services.

Co-operation In cases where a sustained programme of photography is necessary, it may be worth seeking the co-operation of a local camera club, college, or school. Members of a club may have specialist skills which they will be glad to place at the society's disposal, and a college of art, planning or architecture may be interested in undertaking a limited photographic survey as a live project.

Some schools are equipped with cameras and darkrooms and may also be able to help. Even when they are not, it is not a bad idea for a society to suggest that once a year a class should be asked to go out with their (or their parents') cameras to photograph local features which interest, appal, or appeal to them. Almost certainly the outcome will be a new insight into the area's assets and drawbacks, and if the best of the prints can be put on show in the public library, town or village hall, public interest is sure to be aroused.

Applications

Pictorial surveys In all but the smallest villages members—even enthusiastic and knowledgeable members—are unlikely to know what the whole of the society's area looks like. Yet knowledge of a comprehensive kind is essential if a society is to offer well-informed and helpful comment on planning applications and the like. So it helps if a complete *pictorial survey* of the area can be built up and revised when necessary. This should not just be confined to photographs of listed buildings. It should include also views of buildings which perhaps ought to be listed, vistas down key streets or from key vantage-points, panoramic views of waterfronts, hillsides or other features where the skyline is important, illustrations of gap-sites where development may be expected, even perhaps old photographs of buildings which have been mutilated but which one day it may be possible to restore to their original condition.

Listed and listable buildings should be photographed from the rear (and sides) wherever possible, as well as from the front, and some fascinating discoveries may be made in the process, for it is axiomatic that the rear and flank elevations of old buildings often reveal more about their history than the front. There are a surprising number of cases where, for example, a solemn Victorian front camouflages a much older structure. Whenever the opportunity presents itself (for example if the occupier is a member of the society) photographs should be taken of interesting internal features. Particularly in listed buildings there is often a wealth of important features which are unknown to the community at large and have gone unrecorded hitherto.

Prints need only be of ordinary 'enprint' size (3½″×3½″ from square negatives and 3½″×5″ from oblong ones). A good cheap way of storing these compactly for easy reference is to classify them by street, mount them on sheets of foolscap (13″×8″) or A4 duplicating paper, and put them in a lever-arch file. If self-adhesive ring reinforcements are used round the punch-holes, this will eliminate the risk of sheets being wrenched out by mistake. It is best not to stick the prints down but to use transparent photo-corners, so that they can be removed if required. The prints should be properly documented on the reverse, with details of subject, date and negative number, and the negative number should also be written under the mounted print so that if it is temporarily removed it can be returned to its proper place.

Negatives should be carefully filed away, preferably in one of the purpose made albums that are available quite cheaply from photographic dealers. Sooner or later one or other of these negatives will prove absolutely priceless (for example if a damaging and unauthorised alteration is carried out to a listed building and the society wishes to press for restoration) and in any case their value will increase with time for other reasons. The greatest care must therefore be taken of negatives and they must always be handled *only* by the edges.

Colour or black-and-white? Though the price differential is narrowing down, black-and-white is still cheaper, and for a pictorial survey it is quite sufficient, though in the case of particular streets or buildings where the colours of the building materials make a critical contribution to character it is useful to include a few representative close-ups of brickwork, masonry, paving and the like.

Even in a small town probably well over 1,000 prints will be needed for a complete pictorial survey. If the processing is done commercially, this implies a capital outlay of over £100—a sizeable sum for a small or young society. However expenditure can be phased over three or four years if necessary—indeed may have to be anyway if only a single volunteer can carry out the work. In some cases a district council may be willing to subsidise or even underwrite the venture on condition that it receives a copy of every print—many planning officers are keen to possess this kind of survey but lack the staff time to carry it out. Once completed, the pictorial survey will be a priceless asset—and in time of great historic value. It will enable the society to speak with greater authority, particularly if the local authority (as in most cases) has nothing comparable.

And although by definition many of the photographs (taken for record purposes) will lack pictorial quality, sooner or later some of them will come in useful for some of the other purposes described later.

Representations Simply as a basic planning tool, photography can have many applications. A *complaint* to the authorities about a particular problem—say, the illegal use of land as a rubbish dump or car-breaking yard—will carry much greater weight if it can be illustrated with recent photographs. Always better than a mere complaint is a *suggestion* about how a problem might be solved, and here too photography can come in useful. Suppose a society considers a particular type of street-nameplate unsuitable for use in a particular area and wants to suggest the adoption of a style better suited to the setting and already in use in another town nearby. It would be well worth the effort and expense of photographing a few examples of the preferred type and sending these to the highway authority with the society's letter. Black-and-white enprints, provided that they are clear and sharp, should be quite sufficient for the purpose.

Reports Sooner or later most societies want to develop their proposals for the improvement of an area into some kind of *report*. Often this is preceded by a *survey* and accompanied by an *exhibition*. A survey, whether of trees, townscape, eyesores or some other topic, will pack much more punch if it is illustrated. It is not just that a few pictures will leaven the text, nor even that they will serve to illustrate the points it makes: a good picture really is often worth a hundred words.

Here more skill may be required than for a general pictorial survey. The *right* photographs must be included, the *right* vantage-points chosen. 'Cheating' of one kind or another is better avoided. Most people know that with a telephoto lens it is possible to make a street crowded with traffic look positively choked, that with a wide-angle lens a confined space can be made to look almost spacious. But neither lens 'sees' as the human eye sees, and it is better to stick to a standard lens. Otherwise there is a risk that the report or survey may be discredited. Local people will be quick to spot any 'photographic licence' of this kind, while council members and officials will harbour the suspicion that the society's case holds so little water that exaggeration and distortion are the only ways of attracting attention to it. This is not to say that there is no scope for the telephoto or wide-angle lens: the one can be genuinely useful to photograph buildings or details which it is impossible to approach closely with a standard lens; the other, to photograph the facades of buildings in narrow streets.

A few surveys and reports will be printed, most will be duplicated, and some will appear only in typescript, with photocopies for distribution. All typescripts, and many duplicated reports, will be illustrated by original photographs. On grounds of expense the number will therefore have to be limited, and this makes it important to ensure that the best pictures, best size and format, and best method of presentation are adopted. Though small 'enprints' may be sufficient to make some points, or to illustrate several examples of the same problem, half-plate (6½″×4½″) or full-plate (8½″×6½″) prints will make a much bigger impact.

All illustrations should be clearly captioned (with cross-references in the text) and they should never be crowded on the page. Black-and-white prints should be sufficient for most purposes, but colour photographs will be useful when a relevant point needs to be made—for example, about ill-judged colour schemes or new building materials whose tints or tones clash with traditional ones.

Electronic stencils will be needed if photographs are repro-duced in duplicated reports, blocks or plates if they appear in printed ones. Full-plate glossy glazed black-and-white prints are best for these purposes, and since the society is prepared to go to the expense of a longer-run report it is even more important to include only top-quality shots.

Exhibitions The proposals put forward in a report will attract much more attention if an *exhibition* is timed to coincide with publication. Here photographs and other graphic material play the leading role, and so the greatest care must be taken with selection and presentation. The most important rule is not to clog the display space with a proliferation of photographs and a surfeit of text. Not many people have the stamina to absorb and digest such a rich visual stew, but the few with the necessary determination will linger so long that circulation comes to a standstill. So the message must be crisp, the prose spare, and the pictures purposeful.

To be big enough to be viewed without discomfort, prints need to be at least full-plate (6½″×8½″). Photographs 10″×8″ are even better and not much dearer. For really important subjects that need to be highlighted, it may be worth going to the extra expense of one or two prints 16″×12″ or even 20″×15″. Only negatives of the highest quality, taken with a good lens, will be capable of effective enlargement to such a degree. To avoid distracting reflections it is best to obtain matt prints. Impact will be improved if a member with the necessary equipment can dry-mount the prints on card mounts. If a small margin is left round the edges panel-pins can be used to fix the mounted photographs on the display panels. Otherwise photographs should be fixed direct to the boards by pushing chart pins *over* their top and bottom edges—*never* through the corners, as this causes damage and sometimes rust marks.

Press notices A report, exhibition or other major society project is likely to be accompanied by a *press notice*. This is likely to be given greater prominence in the press if it is supported by photographs. The prints should be of tip-top quality, glossy glazed and full-plate sized. A brief caption, suitable for publication without editing, should be typed and stuck on the reverse. The society's name and address needs to be added so that the picture can be returned after use—though some papers may prefer to keep it on file. Black-and-white prints are sufficient, of course. Buttress-envelopes, or ordinary envelopes with a stiff cardboard insert, should be used—otherwise the prints will get bent and cracked in the post.

Public inquiries and national surveys Photographs are often an essential element in a society's submission at a *public inquiry*, to a *Royal Commission* or Government committee or when it participates in a *national survey* such as those on heavy lorries and waste land undertaken by the Civic Trust. The same general rules apply but in the case of a public inquiry it must be borne in mind that prints need to be made available to the other main parties, and the Press, as well as to the Inspector. Colour often comes into its own here, to provide objective evidence of the unique quality of a particular landscape or urban setting.

Picture postcards and slides for sale More and more societies are publishing local-interest *picture postcards, slides* and *Christmas cards*. Pictorial and technical quality need to be high, or the cards and slides simply will not sell. The old trick of 'framing' a building within some foreground element such as a tree, arch or building facade can work wonders by giving a three-dimensional effect. Where the view is of a single building rather than a street, motor vehicles are best eliminated, partly because they spoil the view anyway but also because with their built-in obsolescence they can 'date' a card or slide all too rapidly. It is as well not to be too impatient and to take perhaps a dozen or so shots of the building—at different times of day and year and from different vantage points—before choosing the best for reproduction. Any 'wasted' shots will still be useful in the pictorial survey.

Appendix 5

Informative plaques

Informative plaques as part of a signed trail may be erected on buildings (with the owner's consent) to recall their historical associations or simply to draw attention to their architectural interest.

Plaques more commonly record that a particular famous figure, or figures, lived in a particular house. In a few areas (eg Greater London) they are usually erected by a local authority (eg the Greater London Council) but mostly the initiative is taken by a society or a property-owner. The greatest care is needed to ensure correct identification of the house concerned. Tradition is notoriously unreliable and the evidence of residence must be scrutinised by a member with experience in historical research. Particular pitfalls are that before 1800 not many streets were numbered and that since then many have been re-numbered. Ratebooks (where they survive) and directories (after about 1840) can usually establish an identification beyond doubt. Dates of residence should be included where they can be accurately established.

Because some reputations prove short-lived, it is best not to erect plaques within 20 years of a person's death—and certainly not within their life-time. If not a household name, the person concerned should be someone who is recognised as having made a substantial contribution to human welfare or happiness. If his or her claim to fame, though warrantable, is esoteric, the wording of the plaque should make quite clear what it is—eg 'John Smith, founder of the Peatshire and Loamshire Railway, lived here 1832-1845' or 'Michael Robinson, pioneer of bridge construction in Loamshire, lived here 1782-1799'.

Sometimes the actual house in which a famous figure lived has been replaced by a more recent building. Though a plaque can be erected with the wording 'John Smith . . . lived in a house on this site' it is doubtful whether this has much real value as a means of evoking a link with the past, particularly if the appearance of the whole street has changed. Far better to see if there is not another property, still surviving, to which the plaque can be fixed.

There is no reason why plaques should not record other historical associations, such as surviving factory buildings where significant technical developments took place or old theatres or music halls where famous artistes once appeared. Where a whole street has interesting associations there may be a case for a 'group' plaque at one end recording these.

There may sometimes be a case simply for fixing a plaque to a building to inform passers-by that it is historic, or listed, or a typical 18th century town house, or an important work by a distinguished architect. However there are dangers here. One is that in a historic town with large numbers of listed buildings quite serious visual disruption could be caused by the erection of a plaque on each simply to record that it is listed. And if such plaques were erected only on *some* listed properties, the effect could be positively misleading. Information of this kind is probably better imparted through maps and the printed word.

Great care needs to be taken with the design, manufacture, siting and erection of plaques. The design needs to be such that the plaque can be seen without being obtrusive. If a society plans to erect more than a single plaque they should normally be to a uniform design and colour-scheme. This will aid recognition. To ensure that the plaque is not obtrusive lettering needs to be in white on a darker background that will harmonise with local buildings. Often a neutral shade of grey works well, though in Greater London a mid-blue rather similar to Wedgwood blue has served very well for many years.

Plaques need to be long-lasting and easy to maintain. The most popular materials are glazed stoneware, enamelled steel and cast aluminium. Examples of manufacturers of each are:

Glazed stoneware
Carter & Co (London) Ltd, 157 Clapham Road, London SW9, produce the familiar 'blue plaques' for the Greater London Council. Normally about 19½" in diameter, these are individually designed and made, with Roman lettering. Experience has shown that plaques of this kind have an almost indefinite life expectancy. An additional advantage of the standard blue colour is that, unlike some others used in the past, it does not fade through exposure to sunlight. The cost of manufacture is about £120, and allowance also has to be made for fixing costs, which usually amount to about £60, as masonry has to be cut out to accommodate the plaque, which is about 2" deep.

Enamelled steel

Plaques similar in appearance can be made of stove-enamelled steel, e.g. by Burnham & Co (Onyx) Ltd, Kangley Bridge Road, London SE26. These are cheaper to make (about half the cost of glazed stoneware) and much cheaper to fix, as they can be mounted direct on a facade without cutting out masonry.

Enamelled bronze

Plaques of this kind, though undeniably handsome and durable, are expensive. A rectangular plaque with an eight-line inscription is likely to cost about £400. Mounting (direct on a facade) will cost another £10 or so. One manufacturer is J R Pearson Ltd, of Porchester Street, Birmingham.

Cast Aluminium

These are much the cheapest type. A leading manufacturer, which supplies the Ancient Monuments Branch of the Department of the Environment, the National Trust, the National Trust for Scotland and the Forestry Commission is the Royal Label Factory, College Lane, Stratford-upon-Avon, Warwickshire CV37 6BT. Lettering, which is in relief, can be in a roman or grotesque face. The cost of a typical plaque 12″ in diameter is about £25. Like enamelled steel plaques, these are quite cheap to fix as they can be mounted direct on a building facade.

For most purposes rectangular plaques are preferable to circular ones. Permission for erection on a building will be required from the owner and occupier, and the district council should be consulted to see whether planning or listed building consent is also required.

The siting of plaques needs careful thought, and if possible the advice of an architect should be sought. This is particularly important in the case of listed buildings.

Types of informative plaque (Upper left), the standard pattern 'blue plaque' made in glazed stoneware for the Greater London Council. (Upper right) one of several enamelled bronze plaques erected by York Civic Trust. (Lower left) a cast aluminium plaque installed by Chester Civic trust. Less formal than these – but with its own homespun appeal – is a hand painted (signwritten) plaque in Tewkesbury.

Appendix 6

Some examples of trails already published by local amenity societies

Among the large number of trails already published by local amenity societies the following are among the best.

The information is given in the following order:

—Title, date of publication, and price *exclusive* of postage (Autumn 1978)

— *Size (width×height) and number of pages

— Printing and paper characteristics

— Content and illustrations

— Society and address of Hon Secretary/Publications Officer

Those marked** include brief details of the society responsible

*International standard paper sizes:

A3 420×297mm,
A4 297×210mm,
A5 210×148mm

Area trails in folder form

AMERSHAM: A WALK AROUND THE OLD TOWN 1975 6p
396×210mm folded twice to make 8pp 99×210mm
Black on white cartridge
Straightforward trail with street-plan and 4 line drawings (17th century arcaded market hall on cover)
Amersham Society, 56 First Avenue, Amersham, Bucks. HP7 9BS

TOWN TRAILS: BRUTON, SOMERSET 1977 5p locally (free to other societies)
A4 folded in three to make 6pp 99×210mm
Brown on buff cartridge (designed by West Country Tourist Board)
Town centre trail with street-plan and 5 half-tone blocks from photographs (church and packhorse bridge on cover)
Bruton Town Trust, Southfield House, Bruton, Somerset

CAERLEON HERITAGE TRAIL 1974
A3 folded in half and then once to make 8pp 149×210mm
Four-colour on white coated (produced jointly with local history society and in conjunction with County Planning Officer)
Circular tour round legionary fortress and present-day town, well-illustrated with local and street-plans (both two-colour), 5 colour half-tones, 1 line drawing and 2 monochrome half-tones (Old Tower and quay c 1846 on cover)
Caerleon & Distric Civic Society, 15 Broadwell Court, Caerleon, Gwent

** DEVIZES TOWN TRAIL 1975 15p
750×265mm folded concertina-fashion to 12pp 125×265mm
Black and blue on white coated
Town centre trail with summary of town history on last page: illustrated with street plan and 14 half-tones (Market Cross on cover)
The Trust for Devizes, 51 Avon Road, Devizes, Wilts.

DUDDINGSTON VILLAGE HERITAGE TRAIL 1975 (2nd edition) free
A4 folded in three to make 6pp 99×210mm
Red and black on mustard cartridge (assisted by Scottish Tourist Board)
Village centre trail with location and street plans and 5 line blocks (distant view of church on cover)
Society for the Preservation of Duddingston Village, Lochside House, Duddingston, Edinburgh 15

(EDINBURGH) BLACKET CONSERVATION: AN ADVENTURE TRAIL 1969 10p
432×374mm folded once to make 4pp 216×374mm
Black on pale green cartridge
Short trail through a predominantly 19th-century urban area, with fixed stopping-points. More helpful than most trails in illustrating and explaining architectural details and environmental features. Street-plan (from 1: 25,000 OS plan) and 12 line blocks (street-plan on cover)
The Blacket Association, 23 Blacket Place, Edinburgh 9

ELTHAM TOWN CENTRE WALK 1976 5p
A4 folded in three to make 6pp 99×210mm
Black on white cartridge (very simple offset-litho work)
Straightforward trail through centre of a large village now engulfed by London: street-plan and 5 line blocks (church on cover)
The Eltham Society, 3 Greenacres, The Crescent, Sidcup, Kent

A WALK ABOUT ENFIELD TOWN 1968 5p
339×242mm folded in 3 to make 6 pp 113×242mm
Black and brown on white coated
Town centre trail with street-plan and 15 line blocks (church and market place on cover)
Enfield Preservation Society, 107 Parsonage Lane, Enfield, Middlesex EN2 0AB

A WALK AROUND THE TOWN AND PORT OF FAVERSHAM 1978 (6th edition) free
285×226mm folded in 3 to make 6 pp 93×226mm
Black and brown on white cartridge
Town centre trail with street-plan and 7 line blocks (6 two-colour) (Guildhall and market place on cover)
Faversham Society, Fleur de Lis Heritage Centre, Preston Street, Faversham, Kent ME13 8NS

TOWN TRAIL: CLOCKWISE ROUND THE CITY OF GLOUCESTER 1975 5p
A4 folded in three to make 6pp 99×210mm
Black on white cartridge
Circular city centre trail with all 25 features of interest identified by simple drawings: not typeset but reproduced offset-litho direct from neatly hand-written orginial—an attractive technique (Cathedral on cover)
Gloucester Civic Trust, Tibberton Court, Gloucester GL19 3AF

HISTORIC GLOUCESTER 1977 (3rd edition) 10p
A3 folded in half and then into 3 to make 12pp 99×210mm
Black, blue and orange on white cartridge
47 features of interest on city centre trail: most are illustrated by small but clear drawings printed on street-plan. Some are also identified on a 1712 bird's-eye-view reproduced across 3pp. Details of city history on last page. Generally very accomplished. (Engraving of one of main streets c 1820 reproduced in half-tone on cover).
Gloucester Civic Trust, Tibberton Court, Gloucester GL19 3AF

** A WALK THROUGH OLD LEIGH 1977 10p
412×213mm folded twice to make 8pp 103×213mm
Black on white cartridge (very simple offset-litho work)
32 features of interest on trail through old fishing village now engulfed by Southend-on-Sea: street-plan and 9 line blocks (Creek front on cover)
Leigh Society, 2 New Court, New Road, Leigh-on-Sea, Essex SS9 2EB

A WALK AROUND MONTGOMERY 1976 15p
416×338mm folded in half and then into 4 to make 16pp 104×169mm
Brown and rose on buff cartridge
Handsomely produced town centre trail with isometric street-plan and 9 line blocks (general view to castle ruins on cover)
Montgomery.Civic Society, Tre Llydiant, Montgomery, Powys

THE BUILDINGS OF PENCAITLAND 1977 (2nd edition) free
A4 folded in three to make 6pp 99×210mm
Black on deep rose cartridge
Village centre trail with brief notes on six outlying buildings: simply produced with location and street-plan and 3 line blocks (no illustration on cover)
Pencaitland Amenity Society, Rookwood, Easter Pencaitland, East Lothian

** REIGATE TOWN TRAIL 1975 5p
A3 folded in half and then once to make 8pp 149×210mm
Brown on buff cartridge
Well-produced town centre trail featuring 38 buildings pinpointed on bird's-eye-view spread across 2 pages: 5 line blocks (18th century arcaded Old Town Hall on cover)
Reigate Society, 27 Rushworth Road, Reigate, Surrey RH2 0QF

ROCHESTER: A WALK AROUND THE CITY 1977 (2nd edition) free
354×193mm folded twice to make 8pp 88×193mm
Black, red and yellow on white cartridge
City centre trail with details of other places of interest and one page of local information: street-plan and 4 line blocks (composite view on cover)
Tourist Information Centre, 85 High Street, Rochester, Kent

** A WALK THROUGH SHOREHAM, KENT 1975 10p
A4 folded twice to make 8pp 74×210mm
Black on white cartridge
Simple but elegant village trail with plan, 13 line blocks and 1 half-tone reproduction of painting by Samuel Palmer (who lived in Shoreham) (village street on cover)
Shoreham Society, Bridge Cottage, Shoreham, Sevenoaks, Kent

** A WALK ROUND WARWICK 1976 (2nd edition) 5p
339×212mm folded in three to make 6pp 113×212mm
Black on white cartridge
Simple town centre trail with details of other places of interest: large street-plan across 3 pages and 2 line blocks (Lord Leycester Hospital on cover)
John Gould, 9 High Street, Warwick

Area trails in booklet form

ROUND OLD AYR 1977 (2nd edition) 30p
152×208mm (close on A5), 24pp, centre stapled
Black on white cartridge
Originally produced by Kyle & Carrick Civic Society in conjunction with County Archaeological and Natural History Society
Well-conceived town centre trail with bibliography: street-plan across 2 pages, location plan as in 1480, 8 bold line blocks, and 2 half-tones from old engravings (Auld brig on cover)
Mrs K M Andrew, Reference Library, Carnegie Library, Ayr

BEVERLEY TOWN TRAIL 1975 (2nd edition) 25p
A5 landscape, 36pp, spiral bound
Cover black on mid-blue; text black on white (produced not by a society but by a High School)
Provocative trail with 33 fixed stopping-points at which attention is drawn not only to features of historic interest but also to environmental shortcomings. Users are invited to use their own powers of observation to answer questions—the answers (if needed) are available in the local reference library. They are also given the opportunity of making their own environmental appraisals at particular points. As well as a bibliography lists are included of plants and birds to be 'spotted'. 2 street-plans (from 6" OS map), 1 reproduction of part of 1828 map, 9 line blocks and 1 reproduction of old lithograph (typographical cover)
Beverley High School, Beverley, North Humberside

** A WALK THROUGH BRIDGNORTH 1975 10p
A5, centre stapled, 8pp
Cover black on grey cartridge; text black on white cartridge
Simple but elegantly printed town centre trail with street-plan (only illustration is reproduction of late 19th-century wood engraving of general view on cover)
Bridgnorth Civic Society, 3 Castle Terrace, Bridgnorth, Salop WV16 4AH

A WALK ROUND HISTORIC BURY ST EDMUNDS 1975 20p
A5 landscape, centre stapled, 16pp
Cover and text black on white cartridge
Well-designed town centre trail with street-plan and 17 litho tones from photographs (typical old street on cover)
Bury St Edmunds Society, 6 Southgate Green, Bury St Edmunds, Suffolk

** HASTINGS: WALK ABOUT THE OLD TOWN 1975 30p
100×215mm, centre stapled, 16pp (rear cover folds out to double width)
Cover deep rose on pale grey; text brown on buff
Well-produced trail with street-plan (across inside front cover, 8 half-tones (from watercolours) and 1 line block (fishermen's church—now museum—on cover)
Old Hastings Preservation Society Ltd, 396 High Street, Hastings, Sussex

** HEPTONSTALL HISTORY TRAIL 1976 (6th edition) 25p
145×212mm (close to A5), centre stapled, 32pp
Cover black and brown on white coated; text black on white coated
Comprehensive trail with 46 fixed stopping-points: local plan, street-plan and one other route plan, 26 half-tones (1 from old engraving). So popular that it led to pedestrian congestion along parts of route. (Aerial view of village centre on cover)
Calder Civic Trust, 12 Glen Terrace, Hipperholme, Halifax, West Yorkshire HX3 8EJ

HEXHAM: A VISITOR'S GUIDE 1974 30p
150×215mm (close to A5), centre stapled, 28pp
Cover and text black on white cartridge
Trilingual (English/French/German) trail with 12-fixed stopping-points: street-plan, 7 line blocks and 5 half-tones. 5 pages of advertising. (Market Place on cover)
Hexham Civic Society, 2 Low Close, Eilansgate, Hexham NE46 3EJ

A WALK AROUND KENDAL 1978 (2nd edition) 75p
A4, centre stapled, 26pp
Cover brown and orange on white coated, text black on white coated
Stylish pair of trails with total of 32 fixed stopping-points: accomplished text affording many insights into development of the town, location plan from 1:2,500 OS and other plans drawn to illustrate elevations of buildings on either side of trail routes (in the style of Tallis's 'London Views', c 1840); illustrated by 22 line blocks and half-tones, some from old engravings and photographs. (Photograph of typical Kendal 'yard' on cover)
Kendal Civic Society, Rose Cottage, Entry Lane, Kendal, Cumbria

** HISTORIC WALKS AROUND NOTTINGHAM 1977 25p
A5, centre stapled, 16pp
Cover and text black on white coated
5 separate trails (Medieval Town, Regency Nottingham, Castle Precincts, Georgian Nottingham, Lace Market) with total of 80 fixed stopping-points; street-plan across centre spread and 16 half-tones; useful brief historical introduction. (Council House on cover)
Nottingham Civic Society, 34 Downham Close, Arnold, Nottingham

Theme trails

SCULPTURE IN THE CITY OF GLOUCESTER 1976 5p
A4 folded twice to make 6pp 99×210mm
Black on white cartridge
Theme trail with 34 fixed stopping-points; most sculptures illustrated by small sketches; reproduced offset-litho direct from hand-written original (Bishop Hooper Memorial on cover)
Gloucester Civic Trust, Tibberton Court, Gloucester GL19 3AF

THOMAS OWEN'S SOUTHSEA 1978 (2nd edition) free
380×198mm folded twice to make 8pp 95×198mm
Reddy brown and black on white
Four trails through an early Victorian area created by Thomas Owen, developer, planner and architect; total of 53 fixed stopping-points; street-plan (across 2pp) and 6 line blocks from sketches; brief introduction and bibliography (portrait of Thomas Owen and typical building on cover)
Information Centre, Civic Offices, Guildhall Square, Portsmouth, Hants

Conservation Area Guide

** PLYMPTON ST MAURICE CONSERVATION AREA 1970 10p
141×217mm (close to A5), centre stapled, 12pp
Cover and text black on white coated
Conservation Area trail with four half-tones (2 from photographs, 1 of castle reconstruction drawing, 1 of old manuscript) and street-plan from 25" OS map (listed buildings and Conservation Area boundaries marked) (High Street across covers (back and front))
Plympton St Maurice Civic Association, 57 Fore Street, Plympton St Maurice, Plymouth, Devon

Illustrations